— HOUSE OF —
TUDOR

—HOUSE OF—
TUDOR
A GRISLY HISTORY

MICKEY MAYHEW

PEN & SWORD
HISTORY

AN IMPRINT OF PEN & SWORD BOOKS LTD.
YORKSHIRE – PHILADELPHIA

First published in Great Britain in 2022 by
PEN AND SWORD HISTORY
An imprint of
Pen & Sword Books Ltd
Yorkshire – Philadelphia

ISBN 978 1 39901 104 4

Typeset in Times New Roman 11.5/14 by
SJmagic DESIGN SERVICES, India.
Printed and bound in the UK by CPI Group (UK) Ltd.

Pen & Sword Books Limited incorporates the imprints of Atlas, Archaeology,
Aviation, Discovery, Family History, Fiction, History, Maritime, Military, Military
Classics, Politics, Select, Transport, True Crime, Air World, Frontline Publishing,
Leo Cooper, Remember When, Seaforth Publishing, The Praetorian Press,
Wharncliffe Local History, Wharncliffe Transport, Wharncliffe True Crime and
White Owl.

For a complete list of Pen & Sword titles please contact
PEN & SWORD BOOKS LIMITED
47 Church Street, Barnsley, South Yorkshire, S70 2AS, England
E-mail: enquiries@pen-and-sword.co.uk
Website: www.pen-and-sword.co.uk

Or
PEN AND SWORD BOOKS
1950 Lawrence Rd, Havertown, PA 19083, USA
E-mail: Uspen-and-sword@casematepublishers.com
Website: www.penandswordbooks.com

Contents

Acknowledgements

Authoring a book during a lockdown prompted by a global pandemic has been a real challenge. Nevertheless, I would like to extend my heartfelt thanks to the following institutions for their help during this rather difficult process, and also to the following friends, colleagues and tutors for their inspiration, support and encouragement over the years:

Bodleian Library; The British Library; Chatsworth House; English Heritage; Historic Royal Palaces; Historic Scotland; The National Archives at Kew; National Trust; The Old Hall Hotel in Buxton; from Pen & Sword Books – Claire Hopkins and Alan Murphy; also, Laura Hirst.

Suki Ali; David Allison; Nathen Amin; Ian Beever; Julia Bell; Emily Bennett; Neil Bond; Michele Ceron; Jane Collier; John Deeley-Harkett; Tiffany Durkan; Janice Ferguson; Bob & Chris Forster; Antonia Fraser; Mark Galloway; Paul Gambriel; Geoff Garland; Dan Gifford; Natalie Grueninger; Jane Howard; Christine James; Anna Kennedy; Jamie Lonie; Cate Ludlow; Elisabeth Manson; Graham & Jenny Mayhew; Rosemary Mayhew; Jesse Meza; Jenny Owen; Sue Parry; Bill Penson; Linda Porter; Steve Rattey; Claire Ridgway; Monique Samuels (Collier); Lesley Smith; Shaminder Takhar; Anne Tammelin; Ruth Van Dyke; Alison Weir; Charlie Zahm.

Also, to Steve Forster, for going above and beyond; and to Tiggy, himself now above and beyond.

And to Gary Loveday – gone, but never forgotten.

Foreword by Linda Porter

The fascination with the Tudor dynasty seems unabated. This family, of mixed Welsh and French origin, only occupied the English throne for a little over a hundred years, from the end of the fifteenth century to the beginning of the seventeenth, yet they have captured the imagination in a way that no other royal house can match. They have become a soap opera, embedded, for good or ill, in English consciousness. They are not, of course, British, because they did not rule the entire British Isles. Ironically, it was the line of Margaret Tudor, elder daughter of Henry VII, whose descendants united the crowns of England and Scotland in 1603, an outcome not entirely unforeseen, but still considered a remote possibility, when the thirteen-year-old princess married the king of Scotland, James IV, a century before the death of the last Tudor, Elizabeth I.

Just why the Tudors remain so popular is something of a mystery, even to those historians like myself who have written about them. Perhaps it is because we think we know them, especially Henry VIII and his six wives and 'Gloriana', Elizabeth I, a woman whose ascent to the throne and long reign would surely have astonished her father, had he been able to see the future. And the Tudor industry has spread wide, with podcasts and websites galore, from Australia to the USA. Many are informative, even innovative, but they seldom venture far from the well-trodden paths of popular sentiment. There is a certain comfort in this. After all, weren't the Tudors just like us, but in fancy dress?

The answer to that question is an emphatic no. Early modern people, which is what the Tudors were, lived in a world that was framed very differently from ours. Our secularised, technological age would frighten and appal them. God was at the centre of their lives and the religious differences of the Reformation tore sixteenth-century Europe apart. Elizabeth I may have famously described this as a 'dispute about trifles' but the dispute had ramifications for the security of the State and the obedience of its citizens which no monarch, including the Virgin Queen, could afford to ignore. Henry VIII was able to use the new ideas, which came into England via the European continent, to appoint himself as head of the Church in England, with momentous consequences. Many would suffer for their beliefs, both traditional and new, during his reign and those that followed. The impetus for all this was not any enthusiasm on Henry's part for Protestantism as opposed to the old religion, Catholicism, but his desperation for a male heir.

Amid the eternal emphasis on Henry's wives and Elizabeth's undoubted achievements (though her 'Golden Age' was more tarnished than her admirers care to admit) there is a side to the Tudors that is often overlooked. Theirs was a world of violence, intolerance and ignorance. It was a brutal place to live. Life was cheap and generally short. Disease was rife, exacerbated by the devastation wrought by poor weather on harvests. A very hot or very wet summer meant starvation the following winter. Infant mortality was high and death in childbirth common. The bubonic plague that had killed one third of the population of Europe in the fourteenth century remained an annual threat, smallpox frequently left lifelong scarring where it did not kill outright and previously unknown illnesses like the sweating sickness could kill in a matter of hours. In 1558 an influenza-type virus swept through northern Europe, attacking the well-off more than the poor. It undoubtedly contributed to the death of Mary I and killed off so many bishops that Mary's successor, her sister, Elizabeth, was just about able to push her religious settlement through Parliament, itself badly affected by deaths and absences.

These stark realities were common to all men and women but they were not the only dangers faced by individuals or families vying for position. Ambition could raise you high one minute and send you to the block the next, or see you murdered in cold blood by those you had offended. Forgiveness, a quality in short supply in the sixteenth century, would generally have been viewed as a sign of weakness. Punishments were barbaric, though the nobility were generally spared the worst of them. Decapitation was a merciful end in comparison with being hanged, drawn and quartered or burned alive. Anne Boleyn, Henry's second wife and the undoubted victim of a conspiracy that has still not been entirely unravelled, was almost pathetically grateful for the swordsman from Calais who despatched her in May 1536. Lady Janet Glamis was not so fortunate, being burned at the stake in Edinburgh after she was found guilty of conspiring to poison Henry VIII's nephew, James V of

Scotland. Like Anne Boleyn, the charge was almost certainly without foundation but Janet was the sister of Archibald Douglas, earl of Angus, James V's hated stepfather, then in exile. The king of Scots struck at the family who had blighted his childhood through their sister.

It is this dark underbelly that Dr Mayhew has captured so convincingly in his journey through the Tudor period. This is a relentless story which may surprise the reader who likes the pretty side of the Tudors. But it is also worth remembering that there are contrasting opinions on the people whose misfortunes and cruelties he chronicles here and that the work of many Tudor historians continues to add new dimensions to our understanding of a dramatic period of history. For every horror story related in this book, it is possible to find another side of the Tudor – and Stuart – dynasties. These monarchs were well-educated and accomplished people, interested in literature, art and science, talented musicians and highly effective orators. James IV of Scotland was perhaps the greatest polymath of them all, a man of restless intellect with a great enjoyment of life. Henry VIII was not always a monster. He was an energetic and enthusiastic boy, dancing with such gusto at the wedding of his elder brother, Arthur, to Katherine of Aragon. Henry then was the spare, rather than the heir, and he little thought then that he would become king himself and marry his brother's widow. Mary I, forever remembered as 'Bloody Mary', an epithet which I and other historians have tried hard to counter with a more balanced view of her life and reign, was beloved by her household and godmother to many children, as well as a hard-working head of state. Mary Queen of Scots has been characterised as clueless but her achievements in governing the turbulent cauldron that was Scotland in the first five years of her reign are often overlooked.

This book offers a different perspective on Tudor England. It is a vivid depiction of the dark side of Tudor times. I hope it will inspire the reader to look again at both the glamour and the horror of the period and search more widely for alternative interpretations of the complex personalities that figure in its pages.

Linda Porter, January 2021

Chapter 1

The Routing of Richard III

The Battle of Bosworth, which took place on the 22 August 1485, was to all intents and purposes the beginning of the Tudor reign, an era which would turn out to be perhaps one of the most popular epochs in the whole of English history; certainly, it has become one of the most profitable, at least as far as historians and the producers of various dubious TV dramas and movies are concerned. Indeed, the current public demand for all things Tudor shows no signs of abating. Yet it all began on a humble battlefield in Leicestershire, when Henry Tudor – the future Henry VII – confronted and then killed King Richard III, thereby ending the War of the Roses, the conflict that had cut England apart for so many years, a battle that had been played out between the rival houses of York and of Lancaster.

King Richard III is without doubt one of history's most divisive figures; much-maligned and misunderstood, he is seen by some as the tyrannical, hunchbacked murderer of the poor young Princes in the Tower, and yet the Richard III Society works tirelessly to rehabilitate his tainted image, with varying degrees of success. The recent recovery of his body and the burial it was given were national news for a number of days, during which all of the old debates were rehashed by the various broadcasters, to no apparent conclusion. To put this level of 'adulation' into perspective, it's worth noting that the far more 'popular' Henry VIII – one need only compare their respective film and TV series tallies – has no 'Tudor Society' to fight his corner whatsoever.

Richard III may have been severely lacking in the charm and deportment department, but he had – and still has – dedicated adherents in the droves. As to whether or not he really was a deformed hunchback, access to his skeleton has enabled scientists to discover that his spine was in fact somewhat twisted, but that this may have been caused by a condition called 'adolescent idiopathic scoliosis' rather than any sort of lack of moral fibre. In fact, the idea of Richard III as being deformed both physically and also morally – the two were often intertwined as far as the Tudor mindset was concerned – came for the most part from Shakespeare's 1593 play, named for the controversial king.

Several years after his death, a historian commented that Richard suffered from somewhat 'lopsided' shoulders, a condition consistent with adolescent idiopathic scoliosis. His condition was not so severe that he either limped or suffered from breathing difficulties, as is apparent with some of those who have the condition. He would have been of about average height for the time – between 5ft 5in and 5ft 7in – and fairly active despite his 'deformity'; certainly, he was active enough to ride into the field of battle, even if that choice was to cost him his life. The silhouette of his recovered skeleton can be seen via means of a projection through a glass floor in what is now the King Richard III Visitor Centre, directly above what was once the car park where his body was recovered.

By 1485, the gravest threat to Richard's throne, Henry Tudor, distant scion of the Lancastrian house, had returned from exile in France and landed in Wales, from where he began to gather support and plan his move to supplant the king and claim the crown. Richard, meanwhile, decided to seize the bull by the horns and confront Henry and his forces, with the two sides meeting near Ambion Hill, just south of Market Bosworth, though the *exact* location of the battle, and of Richard's final fall, has been a matter of historical dispute for some time now (matters of historical dispute positively abound where the Tudors are concerned). There are in fact several different memorials to the event, as well as the Bosworth Battlefield Heritage Centre, all of which are set up to mark the occasion and the supposed 'spot' where the king was actually slain.

The whole passage of events – after his death – that led to Richard being buried beneath what eventually became a car park in Leicester is still a matter of some confusion. What seems clear at the start is that Richard believed Henry was riding with an inferior number of troops and so led a headstrong charge against him; after having scored a brief initial victory he was then brutally cut down by Henry's troops in something of a surprise attack. Another source says that after this initial attack Richard actually tried to flee, but his horse became stuck in a marsh and it was at this point that he was set upon and then hacked to death by Henry's men. When his body was eventually recovered from beneath the car park in Leicester in 2012, it was found that there were a considerable number of wounds – nine in all – centred on the skull in particular. Quite why he wasn't wearing a helmet we shall never know, but it seems entirely feasible that he lost it during the course of the battle. The biggest of the blows to his head appeared to have been caused by a halberd – a pole with an axe or a spike on the end – which was used to hack at the back of the head and may have sheared off a large slice of bone in the process; a similar attack had certainly lopped a chunk out of the very top of the king's head. Although there may have been trauma to the body as well, it seems almost certain that it was the blows to the head that actually killed him; several of them sheared right through the skull and actually entered his brain. After Richard fell from his horse, he was set upon by Henry's men, who would have cleaved through his armour until his helmet – if indeed he was wearing one – came off and then rained further blows down upon his unprotected head until he was dead.

Perhaps most painful of all, albeit apparently delivered post-mortem, was the sword thrust up the buttocks as a final show of victory and also of contempt for his reign. Death by means of having not a sword but instead a red hot poker thrust up the anus – as seen in putting down the Pilgrimage of Grace in Showtime's *The Tudors* TV series (2007-2010) – may be more fanciful than factual, although, as one will discover as one reads on, there were scant depths of depravity to which the Tudors would not stoop when it came to punishing the enemies of their regime. That they would have seen fit to degrade the body of Richard III by thrusting a sword up his anus is entirely in keeping with that barely post-medieval mindset.

Following Richard's death, the first of those plentiful – and probably also apocryphal – legends that so frequently follow the Tudors took place: 'the gold circlet Richard wore on his head, over his armour, was knocked off and rolled under a hawthorn bush as his enemies cut him down. The crown was subsequently retrieved by Lord Stanley, who placed it on his stepson's head in a powerful gesture that marked the moment when the Tudor dynasty came into being' (Porter 2013, p39). The wound to the anus would probably have occurred as Richard's body was draped across the back of a horse and taken away to be buried by monks in the grounds of a nearby church. He was just thirty-two years old at the time.

Chapter 2

Catherine of Aragon and the Head of King James IV

Catherine of Aragon, the first of Henry VIII's six wives, was no wallflower when it came to a bit of military warfare. Although she wasn't quite the horsebound warrior of *The Spanish Princess* series (courtesy of Starz), she was certainly capable of holding her own in a military atmosphere, tactically if not tangibly.

Despite her somewhat stubborn, staid reputation as a matronly monarch prone to turning the other cheek to Henry's occasional infidelities, Catherine was still the daughter of Ferdinand and Isabella of Spain, the mighty monarchs who between them helped to hold the balance of power in Europe for several years. And so it was, in 1513, when the young Henry VIII went off to make war with France – as he frequently did – that he had enough confidence in his wife's abilities to leave her as regent of England in his stead. The Scots – old enemies of the English – saw this as an opportune moment to sneak south across the border with their king, James IV, at their head, with the intent to make an awful lot of mischief for the English. This was in spite of the fact that a peace had been concluded between the two countries in recent years, cemented by the wedding of Henry's elder sister, Margaret, to James. This line of descent would culminate in further trouble for the Tudor regime with Margaret's granddaughter, Mary Queen of Scots.

By causing such consternation for the English forces already encamped in France, James was primarily aiding Scotland's old allies. All of this was done despite James IV having apparently been beset by a ghostly vision dressed in blue, which confronted him as he prayed for guidance in St Michael's Church at Linlithgow Palace. The spectre sought to dissuade him from what it warned would be a potential disaster if he carried on with his plan to invade England. James, however, ignored the warning and went ahead with his plan.

4

By way of a response to his challenge, Catherine of Aragon donned full armour and made a rallying speech to the assembled English troops, despite being pregnant at the time. She also issued a warrant that decreed that all of the properties of Scotsmen in England should be immediately seized by the Crown. Her sometimes director of studies, Peter Martyr, commented on her prowess: 'and on 23 September reported that Catherine, "in imitation of her mother Isabella", had made a splendid speech to the English captains. She told them "to be ready to defend their territory, that the Lord smiled upon those who stood in defence of their own, and that they should remember that English courage excelled that of all other nations"' (Starkey 2004, p145).

The Scots eventually met the English in Northumberland near the village of Branxton. The Scots had in fact been stationed near Flodden Field – hence the name given to the battle – but that was not the actual location of the main thrust of the battle, which is also referred to by a few as 'The Battle of Branxton'. The English scored a spectacular victory and the Scots were utterly defeated; it wouldn't be the last time, either. James IV was killed in the fight, having apparently been hacked down after a disastrous charge in much the same fashion that Richard III had been slain. Upon securing this crushing victory against the Scots, Catherine promptly decided to send James' head to Henry as both a souvenir and also as a proof of her resounding victory over the invading forces. Her letter was as follows, in which she was canny enough to credit the victory against the Scots to her husband and his monumental ego, rather than to herself:

Sir,

My Lord Howard hath sent me a letter open to your Grace, within one of mine, by the which you shall see at length the great Victory that our Lord hath sent your subjects in your absence; and for this cause there is no need herein to trouble your Grace with long writing, but, to my thinking, this battle hath been to your Grace and all your realm the greatest honour that could be, and more than you should win all the crown of France; thanked be God of it, and I am sure your Grace forgetteth not to do this, which shall be cause to send you many more such great victories, as I trust he shall do. My husband, for hastiness, with Rougecross I could not send your Grace the piece of the King of Scots coat which John Glynn now brings. In this your Grace shall see how I keep my promise, sending you for your banners a king's coat. I thought to send himself unto you, but our Englishmens' hearts would not suffer it. It should have been better for him to have been in peace than have this reward. All that God sends is for the best.

My Lord of Surrey, my Henry, would fain know your pleasure in the burying of the King of Scots' body, for he has written to me so. With the next messenger your Grace's pleasure may be herein known. And with this I make an end, praying God to send you home shortly, for without this no joy here can be accomplished; and for the same I pray, and now go to Our Lady of Walsingham that I promised so long ago to see. At Woburn the 16th of September.

I send your Grace herein a bill found in a Scotsman's purse of such things as the French King sent to the said King of Scots to make war against you, beseeching you to send Mathew hither as soon as this messenger comes to bring me tidings from your Grace.

Your humble wife and true servant, Katharine.

However, the English court was horrified by what it saw as a blatant sign of barbarity and disrespect. Beheadings during battle were one thing but mailing the results first class overseas was apparently too distasteful, even for them. Catherine was therefore dissuaded from the idea and had to make do merely with sending a piece of the Scottish king's bloodstained coat to her husband instead. She was then discreetly informed that it might be best if she didn't boast too much about her stupendous victory over the Scots, as Henry had himself scored a success against France and it wasn't seen as wise – in a ponderously patriarchal society – for a wife to try and eclipse her husband's manly victory, even with the very best of intentions. On this occasion at least, Catherine of Aragon listened to the advice that she was given.

As for the body of the fallen Scots king, well, plans were made initially for it to be buried in the monastery of Sheen in Richmond-

Upon-Thames. However, because James had been excommunicated from the Church, partly due to breaking the 1502 Treaty of Perpetual Peace between England and Scotland, and also because of his support for the French against their war with the papacy (England was, at the time, very much considered a papal ally), his body was left to rot in one of the woodsheds at the monastery in Sheen, even after the Pope had given permission for it to be given a proper, consecrated burial. For several decades the body was left all but abandoned, during which time the head apparently became detached from the torso. This may have happened during the slaughter, because it ties in with the fact that Catherine of Aragon seemed to think it a viable option in mailing it to her husband while he was in France. Legend has it that some workmen then used the head as a football, before it was retrieved by the master glazier of Elizabeth I, who took it home with him, as one does when one finds an unattached head rolling around in a public place. After that, the head was – at some further point – dumped in the charnel pit at the church of Great St Michael in the City of London (a charnel pit is a room or crypt – quite often within the bowels of a church – where various 'loose' human remains are stored, often those found buried in the nearby earth while fresh graves are being dug).

The monastery in Sheen was eventually demolished and replaced with a golf course, which means that the headless body is still there, somewhere, waiting to be rediscovered in much the same manner as was the body of Richard III. The church of Great St Michael was also eventually demolished and the site is now occupied by a pub. The chances of both body and head being recovered – and perhaps at some point being reunited – remains rather slim. James IV simply doesn't appear to have the 'fan following' of Richard III. Furthermore, the Scots have a habit of leaving the bodies of their fallen kings where they lay. The mummified corpse of the third husband of Mary Queen of Scots, the Earl of Bothwell, is still in the vicinity of Dragsholm Castle in Denmark, where he was imprisoned in the last years of his life. A husk referred to as 'Bothwell's Mummy' was displayed in the Edinburgh Wax Museum from 1976, although the provenance of the body has never been satisfactorily explained.

Chapter 3

The Fall of Cardinal Wolsey

Despite his 'humble' beginnings as the son of an Ipswich butcher, Cardinal Thomas Wolsey rose so high in the court of Henry VIII that it was said that it was actually he himself who ran England, while his lord and master spent his days hunting, jousting, and bedding various members of the Boleyn family. But when it came to securing the king a divorce from his first wife Catherine of Aragon, Cardinal Wolsey would find that his legendary luck had in fact run dry. Basically, he found himself facing a papacy that sought to prolong the proceedings to the point that Henry eventually lost his patience and cut himself free of Catholicism once and for all. It seems that the papacy had been hoping that he might perhaps return to his wife instead, but by this time Henry's patience – not to mention his virility – was running dry.

What of course did happen in the end was that Henry broke with Rome and appointed himself head of the Church in England. One may possibly view this as being England's first go at a sort of Brexit, although the whim was all the monarch's and not that of the public. Such a move, however, meant disaster for England's premier prelate, i.e., Cardinal Wolsey. Losing the divorce for his monarch meant that Wolsey was left to face the full enmity of the Boleyn faction, and particularly the personal malice of 'the night crow' Anne Boleyn – his own personal nickname for her – who also had a personal score to settle with Wolsey on account of the fact that he'd once foiled her engagement to Henry Percy, the future Earl of Northumberland. Certainly, Wolsey had a lot more to fear from Anne Boleyn than he did from Catherine of Aragon, as Inigo de Mendoza (a diplomat in the service of Charles V, the Holy Roman Emperor) was aware of: 'Mendoza was equally clear what a threat to Wolsey's power Anne would be as Henry's wife, unlike the present queen "who can do him little harm"' (Ives 2004, p110). As Thomas Cromwell would also later learn, to please Henry VIII was to find yourself on to a winner; to piss him off was to effectively place your head on the execution block and give the headsman carte blanche to hack away at your neck and shoulders to his heart's delight.

The hearing into the divorce between Henry and Catherine of Aragon was held at Blackfriars Church, wherein the queen famously fell to her knees in front of the king and begged him for mercy, given that she was 'just a poor woman alone and with no friends in a foreign land', and how she had tried her best to be friends with the king's friends even though she didn't much care for the company that he kept.

Much of the talk during the hearing had then centred around the lurid details of whether or not Catherine's first marriage in 1501, to Henry's older brother, Arthur, had in fact been consummated. Various eyewitnesses were brought forth into the court at Blackfriars to give out their little soundbites in favour of the fact that Catherine was anything other than the virgin she claimed to be, such as the fact that Arthur had apparently emerged from his bedchamber on the morning after his wedding night to proclaim to all within earshot that 'last night I had been in the midst of Spain!' In Tudor times, bloodstained bedsheets were seen as a sure sign of a successful evening where a virginal bride was concerned, but apparently, and despite Arthur's boasting, there were none to be seen. Historians – not to mention the Blackfriars court itself – have thus agonised over whether or not Catherine was a virgin when she left her marriage bed – she maintains that she was – or whether or not she and Arthur did in fact enjoy some semblance of a physical relationship before his untimely death.

When the representatives from Rome decided on a period of prolonged procrastination from the court proceedings, it soon became clear that Wolsey's days were numbered. It was at the end of the aforementioned proceedings – or near enough – that a dumbstruck Wolsey was scolded by Charles Brandon, who commented to him that 'it was never merry in England whilst there were cardinals amongst us', or words to that effect. Basically, Wolsey had fallen so far that Henry's best friend saw fit to give him a scolding, and still worse was to come.

After Wolsey's failure to persuade the papacy to secure the divorce, Henry VIII first toyed with his disgraced cardinal for a while, sending him small tokens of esteem and affection, but eventually Wolsey was arrested and stripped of all the symbols of his great office. The first attempt to do this, with the Dukes of Norfolk and Suffolk in attendance and delighting in his downfall, had Wolsey sending them away because they didn't have the necessary permission to relieve him of the great seals of his office. But it was only a temporary respite, and a pyrrhic victory at that. He was, however, allowed to keep his title and position of Archbishop of

York and it was there that he retired after his disgrace, although he was soon arrested for treason by none other than Henry Percy. Karma could be a terrible bitch, even in Tudor times, and especially when you had Anne Boleyn behind the scenes but pretty much firmly in the driving seat. This particular portion in Wolsey's life has recently been covered in great detail by Hilary Mantel in *Wolf Hall*, and in subsequent BBC adaptation, with Jonathan Pryce playing Wolsey with considerable *élan*.

Wolsey was escorted back to London in disgrace, perhaps to face the full horrors of a traitor's death, but in fact died at Leicester during one of the many stopovers, having fallen ill from a combination of disease and – the far more probably culprit – distress. The season finale to series one of Showtime's *The Tudors* TV series had him exiting this mortal plane in far more dramatic style, slashing his own throat with a knife that had perhaps rather foolishly been provided for his food. The subsequent scenes then showed a shocked Henry VIII swearing that the truth about his demise must remain forever a secret. Now, such a scenario is not completely out of the question, but given Catholic views on suicide it does seems rather unlikely that Wolsey really did decide to take his own life in order to avoid someone else taking it on his behalf. If, however, this was in fact the case then it may all have come down to how much he feared the horror of being hung, drawn and quartered before a baying crowd, for whom an execution was considered the modern equivalent of a good day out at Chessington World of Adventures.

Given the enormity of cover-ups and suppressed scandals that dog the present-day echelons of power, it isn't unreasonable to suppose that there might be a fair few Tudor tales that were carefully tucked under the nearest Turkish rug, never to see the light of day. Some people call them conspiracy theories, whereas others consider them simply documents waiting to be discovered. However, it seems more likely that fear finished Cardinal Wolsey off – the fear of Henry VIII's wrath, especially with Anne Boleyn whispering sweet suggestions into his ear.

Today, there is a bronze statue of Cardinal Wolsey in his hometown of Ipswich, crafted by the renowned sculptor David Annand. It can be found at the junction of Silent Street and St Peter's Street, close by to the spot where it is believed that Wolsey lived as a young man. The statue has a cat peering from behind the robes, while Wolsey himself sports an open, outstretched hand, one that is often found to be holding an empty beer can on a Sunday morning, courtesy of a cheeky reveller who passed by the night before.

Chapter 4

Bishop Fisher's Bad Broth

Bishop John Fisher of Rochester – later made a cardinal by the Pope for his efforts in opposing what Rome viewed as the increasing tyranny of Henry VIII – was a staunch supporter of Catherine of Aragon in her divorce battle with Henry. Alongside Thomas More, Bishop Fisher viewed with increasing horror the idea that Henry VIII should declare himself head of the Church in England, effectively cutting the entire country off from the succour of Catholicism. Bishop Fisher was therefore viewed with some considerable degree of hostility by the Boleyn faction, especially as Anne Boleyn's influence over an infatuated Henry was increasing to an almost overwhelming level on a daily basis… What Anne wanted Anne got, unless it happened to be a speedy divorce for her sweetheart.

Bishop Fisher was in his late fifties when the 'King's Great Matter' first reared its head, appearing in the defence of Catherine of Aragon at the Blackfriars court proceedings regarding the royal divorce. When it became clear that matters were spiralling out of control, he also apparently conspired to have England invaded so that Henry might be overthrown, with the religious life of the country then put quickly back on its proper course. These plans came to nothing, and they exist now merely as one of those amusing and curious byways of English history, when it is possible to ponder on what the whole amazing Tudor epoch would have been like had matters gone in a different direction, with Henry and Anne being overthrown in the midst of their maddened mutual passion.

In 1531, during the height of the tensions regarding the 'King's Great Matter', a cook – one Richard Roose (or Rouse) – was persuaded to add some sort of a poisonous substance to the porridge or broth that Bishop Fisher and his household were soon to be eating. After such a span of time, we have no way of knowing what particular substance was used, but it may have been simply common ratsbane – ratsbane, also known as white arsenic, was commonly used during Tudor times. However, it may have been something a little more 'exotic', such as henbane. Henbane, often rather fetchingly known as 'stinking nightshade', is a highly toxic plant with psychoactive qualities, to which, rather strangely, pigs are said to be entirely immune. Some of the symptoms of henbane poisoning include a dry mouth, convulsions, vomiting, blurred vision and delirium. Then again, it may have been a sprinkling of wolfsbane that did the trick. Wolfsbane is so toxic that the ancient Romans actually used it as a method of execution, and hunters have in times past tipped their arrows in the stuff in order to completely incapacitate their prey. For humans, symptoms of wolfsbane poisoning might include convulsions, nausea and vomiting, alongside confusion and also mania. Either way, when the meal was finally consumed, several of Fisher's servants died as a result. Fisher himself survived only because, in the words of Thomas More in the opening episode of season two of *The Tudors*, 'Bishop Fisher himself ate so little of the broth.'

There seems to be a sprinkling of fact in that particular line of the script. One has only to read contemporary accounts of Bishop Fisher – described as 'skeletal' – to imagine how parsimonious he might be where his appetite was concerned. That particular episode of the popular TV series also showed Richard Roose being paid to commit the heinous crime by none other than Thomas Boleyn, Anne's father, with her brother George giving Roose the poison in rather a peculiarly shaped little vial. In real life – as on TV – Roose was soon apprehended and placed under interrogation in the Tower of London, whereupon he said that he had thought the substance he had added to the meal were simply laxatives and that the whole thing was therefore meant as a practical joke. However, this story didn't wash terribly well with his accusers. The crime of poisoning was so feared in Tudor times that the terrible punishment of being boiled alive – usually in oil – was passed as a deterrent. To give an idea of how much people feared being done away with by poisoning, tasters for the various dishes and delicacies were often employed by royalty to sample the food before they then consumed it themselves. Quite how modern health and safety would have tackled the legalities and logistics of such a profession these days rather boggles the mind.

In accordance with the law and having been found guilty of the crime of poisoning, Richard Roose was boiled to death on 5 April 1531 at Smithfield, whereby he was first swathed in chains and then attached to a hoist mechanism. He was then hoisted upwards from a small wooden platform and lowered into what was either a heated cauldron or perhaps a large kettle. A merciful death meant that the victim was lowered in head-first, but if the executioner had been ordered to prolong the agony then a victim could be lowered in feet-first – not to mention ever so slowly – and then even pulled out a few times so that they might suffer even longer, rather like dunking a biscuit several times in a hot cup of tea. There is no record as to which particular way Richard Roose met his fate, but that self-same episode of *The Tudors* seems to indicate that he went in feet-first, with Nick Dunning's dastardly Thomas Boleyn looking on, his lips quivering in sadistic appreciation.

The winch mechanism which allowed for such a terrible technique was perhaps inspired by a similar form of burning that was employed in France at roughly the same period, whereby a special apparatus was set up so that the victim might be slowly roasted over the flames as opposed to simply standing in the midst of them while tied to a stake. At irregular intervals the apparatus was employed and the victim was hoisted back out of the flames before being 'turned over' and lowered back in, rather like turning over some chicken escallops in the frying pan. Another French punishment for the crime of poisoning was to tie the victim flat out on the ground with each of his limbs bound to a different horse. At a given signal the horses would be startled and would then bolt, taking the unfortunate victim's arms and legs with them. Following on from this multiple dismemberment, rapid death from blood loss or outright shock was soon to follow.

The actual brains behind the attempt on Bishop Fisher's life were never brought to book, if indeed there were any. Perhaps Richard Roose himself was an ardent supporter of the divorce and sought to hasten matters in his own particular manner by despatching Bishop Fisher, or perhaps he really was paid by the Boleyn family to remove Bishop Fisher from the table, quite literally. Perhaps a particular person from the aforementioned family had a direct hand in it instead: 'whether or not she [Anne Boleyn] was guilty can, of course, never be proved. That she was quite capable of it, though, is strongly suggested by a message she sent to Fisher in October 1531. She advised him meaningfully not to attend parliament in case he should have a repetition of the sickness he had previously suffered' (Bruce 1972, p178).

Anne Boleyn's supporters are so many and so ardent that such a slur simply will not be countenanced, but in the context of the crimes it is not altogether out of the question. This was the same woman who whispered malicious nothings into Henry VIII's ear until Thomas More was executed, and who threatened to box the ears of Catherine of Aragon's daughter Mary 'like the bastard she was' if she didn't kowtow to the new order of things. That Anne had previously connived in the downfall of Cardinal Wolsey has already been amply illustrated, but there now exists such a cult of panegyric about her that it seems doubtful that such accusations of poisoning will seriously stick, although her father's legacy is always ripe for more of a realistic bashing. Watch any TV series or film concerning Thomas Boleyn and you'll bear witness to the varying different ways in which he can be portrayed as a heartless, scheming bastard, although Nick Dunning did it best.

Chapter 5

The Sweating Sickness

The Sweating Sickness was one of the most dreaded of all the diseases of the Tudors, one that plagued both the palace and the public during the late-fifteenth and sixteenth centuries (leprosy came a close second but was more common in continental Europe than it was in England). The Sweating Sickness – or 'The Sweat', as it was sometimes shortened to – could strike a person dead within hours and lay waste to entire communities as it raged around the larger towns and cities, which it often did. When compared to the 'slow burn' and lower mortality rate of COVID-19, it's clear to see why the Tudor public lived in such benighted dread of another outbreak. The first actual recorded instance was around 1485 – the same year as the Battle of Bosworth – and from then on lasted with regular visitations until roughly 1551, when the last cases were said to have occurred. The Sweating Sickness outbreaks were almost always during the summer, whereas strains of virus such as COVID-19 tend to claim more victims during the colder months.

It certainly didn't help the all-consuming fear at the merest mention of the Sweating Sickness that one of the first symptoms was said to be an awful feeling of apprehension and dread on the part of the afflicted. Cold shivers followed shortly after, followed by dizziness and aches and pains in all of the limbs. It was then that the sweating itself would begin, and by that stage the sufferer would know for sure that death would soon come knocking upon their flimsy wooden door. The final stage of would see an almost complete bodily collapse, alongside an overwhelming urge on the part of the victim to lay down and sleep, something of which the 'doctors' of the time insisted would prove fatal. At this point patients were slapped or had water thrown in their faces to try and keep them awake, in an effort to bring them through the final stage of the disease without actually perishing.

Some people did in fact survive an attack of the Sweating Sickness, Cardinal Wolsey among them. Anne Boleyn also survived a particularly virulent outbreak in 1528, when some 2,000 people died in London alone. Anne Boleyn's brother-in-law, William Carey, husband to Mary *'The Other Boleyn Girl'* Boleyn, died during that outbreak, as did one of the king's favourites, Sir William Compton. On this occasion Henry VIII fled both the capital and also the 'pretty duckies' (breasts) of Anne Boleyn, sending one of his top physicians to treat her while she lay suffering within the confines of Hever Castle. Thomas Cromwell's wife and two daughters also lost their lives during or shortly after this outbreak.

Tudor life, on the whole, was often short, harsh and brutal, and people were in a sense inured to loss in a way that modern sensibilities would find hard to fathom. One can merely marvel at the constitution of a man like Thomas Cromwell, who could pick himself up after such a loss and continue to the point where he became the man running the country on behalf of Henry VIII.

Modern medicine remains rather stumped as to the origins, causes, and also the true nature of the Sweating Sickness. There has been some speculation that it may have been brought over from France by Henry Tudor's men ahead of the Battle of Bosworth, where one of the first cases was recorded, and where it laid waste to a sizeable number of people when the triumphant new king entered into London after the defeat of King Richard III.

It may be that the Sweating Sickness was a disease similar in nature to the hantavirus pulmonary syndrome, which is caught from infected mice, rats, and voles. Anthrax has also been cited as another possible culprit for the condition. But this is all speculation. Famed Tudor historian Alison Weir said of the disease that 'it is impossible to be certain what the "sweating sickness" actually was, as no cases were reported after the last outbreak in 1551. Some have speculated that it was a military fever such as malaria, or a particularly virulent form of "prickly heat", or even what later came to be known as "trench fever", while another suggests it was a strain of influenza or typhus, or "a viral infection transmitted by rats"' (Weir 2011, p175). By the time Henry and Anne's daughter, Elizabeth I, was on the throne, there seems to have been a decrease in the general anxiety regarding the Sweating Sickness, which tallies with the fact that one of the last recorded cases was in 1551, several years before the Virgin Queen ascended the throne.

Besides the Sweating Sickness, various other maladies – many of them still common to the modern ear – were rife, including typhoid, dysentery and various forms of influenza, as well as leprosy. A general lack of hygiene meant that even a cut on the finger could quickly lead to infection and death. It seems remarkable therefore that anyone even made it into adulthood in Tudor times, though many certainly did.

Chapter 6

Pride Comes Before a Fall: Thomas More

Up until the advent of Henry VIII's divorce from Catherine of Aragon, or 'The King's Great Matter', as it came to be called, the king enjoyed a close companionship – in fact one might almost venture to call it a fully-fledged friendship – with the lawyer and Renaissance humanist Thomas More. In fact, Charles Brandon aside, More was pretty much the king's best friend during the early years of his reign. They went up onto the roof of Hampton Court Palace together to talk about the patterns of the stars, and Henry even visited More at his family home in Chelsea and begged him to take a permanent place at court, something that More always declined. The backbiting and the gossip weren't to his more refined tastes, by all accounts. In his own words, More was under no illusions whatsoever that while Henry appeared to favour him, he would have his head off his shoulders in a moment if it might secure him a castle in a foreign land.

Thomas More was a man ahead of his times in many respects, a man who believed strongly in the education of women, for one thing. His daughter Margaret was a prime example of his desire to advance all of his children equally and he positively doted on her in this regard, producing one of the most eloquent women ever to bestride the Tudor stage. However, More was still a product of his patriarchal times and he still believed in the Biblical supremacy of male over female, and in this regard he was particularly cruel to his first wife; his second wife he seems not even to have shared a bed with, as such.

He famously wrote the book *Utopia*, in which he imagined a perfect future society set on a remote island that was free from all forms of corruption. But despite his well-educated demeanour, More was also a violent, almost savage opponent of the new Protestant movement that was sweeping through Europe at the time. When he eventually landed the position of Lord High Chancellor of England he used his new powers to burn many heretics at the stake. These burnings were, with what seems like some sort of awful, macabre pun, all 'well done'. It would prove to be a dreadful example as a way of rooting out heresy, one that Henry VIII's daughter Mary would take to even more shocking extremes when she ascended to the throne some twenty-odd years later. Thomas More burned books as well as heretics, whereas his predecessor, Cardinal Wolsey, had, on occasion, been more content to turn the occasional blind eye to the latter and settled simply for toasting the former.

It has also been rumoured that Thomas More tortured heretics in a concealed dungeon in the bowels of his Chelsea home, either on the rack or by some other means, and that he kept them there in chains for weeks at a time and without proper recourse to the letter of the law. Historians partial to More have downplayed or even denied this aspect of his life, but even medieval mud sticks, and the accusations remain a stain on his reputation to this day. The play and the film *A Man for All Seasons* (a movie that the Vatican has insisted is one of the greatest cinematic masterpieces of all time) tend to skip past these slightly less salubrious sides to More's legacy, instead focusing on him as the man who attempted to oppose the tyranny of Henry VIII as he tore England away from the comforting fold of Rome in order to marry his concubine (Anne Boleyn). This scenario makes Thomas More the perfect Catholic martyr, and that is exactly what he became when his friendship with the king dissolved and he found himself standing almost alone in opposition to Henry's wishes.

It is important to understand that in Tudor times religious intolerance was not only prevalent, but was also actively encouraged, and in this regard Thomas More was something of a monarch himself. In fact, the bravery he showed in standing up to Henry VIII is nothing sort of astonishing, especially when one takes into account that Cardinal Wolsey may have been quite literally scared to death at the thought of facing Henry's wrath. When Henry began his affair with Anne Boleyn – which led to his separation from Catherine of Aragon, his petition for a divorce and finally his eventual break with Rome, then setting himself up as the head of a new English Church – it was then that Thomas More promptly retired from his role as Lord High Chancellor. He returned to his Chelsea home and did his best to keep his head beneath the proverbial parapet, until he was required to emerge into the light of day and sign the newly inscribed Act of Succession, acknowledging Henry's new role as head of the English Church.

For refusing this simple task of soliciting his immortal soul, Thomas More was cast into the Tower of London (the Bell Tower, to be specific). His family – his beloved daughter Margaret in particular – frequently visited him while he was there and pleaded with him to sign the act, but More's mind had already fast-tracked itself to the status of martyrdom – something he finally achieved when he was canonised in 1935 – and so he simply sat back and awaited the inevitable trial to come. Before and also while all of this was going on, it became pretty clear that England's potential new queen was calling for his head: 'Anne was constantly urging the king to put them to death, and "when the Lady wants anything, there is no one who dares contradict her, not even the King himself"' (Weir 2007, p281). More may have been threatened with torture – some may have considered it a salutary taste of his own medicine – but there is no record that he was ever coerced in such a fashion.

The trial itself took place at Westminster Hall – the spot is now clearly marked with a plaque – and following the guilty verdict, More was sentenced to suffer the full horrors of a traitor's death of being hung, drawn and quartered. The king, however, commuted the sentence to a simple beheading, and so it was that Thomas More was led to the scaffold on Tower Hill – the site is also clearly marked – on a decidedly wet and dismal day on 6 July 1535. His last letter, written to his beloved daughter Margaret the day before, reads as follows:

Our Lord bless you.

My dearly beloved daughter, good daughter and your good husband, and your little boy, and all yours, and all my children, and all my godchildren, and all our friends. Recommend me when you may to my good daughter Cecily, whom I beseech our Lord to comfort. I send my blessing to her and to all her children and pray her to pray for me. I send her an handekercher and God comfort my good son her husband. My good daughter Daunce hath the picture in parchment that you delivered me from my Lady Coniers; her name is on the back side. Show her that I heartily pray her that you may send it in my name again for a token from me to pray for me.

I like special well Dorothy Coly, I pray you be good unto her. I would wit whether this be she that you wrote me of. If not, I pray you be good to the other as you may in her affliction and to my good daughter Joan Aleyn to give her I pray you some kind answer, for she sued hither to me this day to pray you be good to her.

I cumber you good Margaret much, but I would be sorry, if it should be any longer than tomorrow, for it is Saint Thomas eve, and the Vtas of Saint Peter and therefore tomorrow long I to go to God, it were a day very meet and convenient for me. I never liked your manner toward me better than when you kissed me last, for I love when daughterly love and dear charity hath no leisure to look to worldly courtesy.

Farewell my dear child and pray for me, and I shall for you and all your friends that we may merrily meet in heaven. I thank you for your great cost.

I send now unto my good daughter Clement her algorism stone and I send her and my good son and all hers God's blessing and mine.

I pray you at time convenient recommend me to my good son John More. I liked well his natural fashion. Our Lord bless him and his good wife my loving daughter, to whom I pray him be good, as he hath great cause, and that if the land of mine come to his hand, he break not my will concerning his sister Daunce. And our Lord bless Thomas and Austen and all that they shall have.

In stark contrast, his last words to the lieutenant of the Tower were apparently along the lines of, 'I pray you, I pray you, Mr Lieutenant, see me safe up and for my coming down, I can shift for myself.' Therefore, it was quite clear to the onlookers that Thomas More could keep his head even when it was about to be struck off.

Chapter 7

The Miscarriages of Anne Boleyn

Henry VIII's new queen, Anne Boleyn, was supposed to bring about a golden reign to England, ending Catherine of Aragon's disappointing string of stillbirths and high infant mortality rate by giving birth to the son that England – not to mention Henry VIII – so desperately craved. The fact that their first child was a girl – the future Elizabeth I – was a crushing disappointment, but not a total defeat for Anne Boleyn and her somewhat worried womb. After the birth – and the significantly toned-down celebrations that were soon to follow – Henry assured her that they were both still young, and that with God's grace boys would soon follow. This would, in his patriarchal mindset, compensate for the disappointment of having yet another daughter to barter about the foreign princes of Europe once she was old enough to be wed. The only problem was that boys didn't follow for Anne Boleyn, or when they did they were miscarriages, and each one of those miscarriages saw the chances of her own survival slip further and further away. In the meantime, all manner of astrologers were consulted – it had been predicted that her first pregnancy would result in a male child – and quite possibly various other routines and remedies were applied in order to steer each successive pregnancy in the appropriate direction.

Elizabeth Tudor was born on the 7 September 1533. It hadn't been a particularly pleasant pregnancy for Anne Boleyn but it had presented no great problems either. The child had most likely been conceived when the royal couple were stranded in Calais, awaiting a fair wind to bring them back to England after a successful visit to the French court. In early 1534 it was reported that the queen was pregnant again, but then in the summer all rumoured mentions of this new pregnancy abruptly ceased, as though it had never been at all. It is possible that Anne Boleyn had suffered a miscarriage during the summer of that year; either that or it was a phantom pregnancy brought about by the desire to furnish the country with the male heir she so fervently sought. Certainly, she was under considerable pressure to produce the aforementioned male heir she had so passionately promised to the king, and that pressure would only have intensified with the birth of Elizabeth.

It is interesting to speculate what might have become of Anne Boleyn had she successfully given birth to another live female child. Had she in fact produced a second daughter after Elizabeth then the marriage may have lasted another few years longer than it did, but unless she stumped up a son then most likely she would still have gone the way that she did. Of course, if she had produced a live son after Elizabeth then she would have been virtually untouchable. Matters in 1534, however, were not helped by the fact that it appeared that Henry's attentions were wandering away from his once-beloved new wife: 'Relations between the royal couple were not at all satisfactory just then. Once again, at the end of Anne's last pregnancy, the King had been unfaithful. Chapuys reported that the object of Henry's desire was "a very beautiful and adroit young lady for whom his love is daily increasing". She was probably one of the Queen's ladies, but her name is unknown' (Weir 2007, p272). In *The Tudors*, this phantom female is given the name of 'Lady Eleanor Luke'.

Another pregnancy for the queen was reported in 1535, ahead of the one that culminated in Anne's tragic miscarriage on 29 January 1536, but this one is even more shadowy than the pregnancy of 1534. It may be that there was simply a letter referring to that first pregnancy in 1534, following on from the birth of Elizabeth, which was erroneously marked as belonging to 1535, when details were even harder to come by. Either way, Henry and Anne went on progress during the latter half of 1535, a tour that included the 'famous 'stop-off at Wolf Hall, home of the Seymour family. Far from being the turning point in their relationship that so many observers have morbidly claimed, this was in fact almost certainly the point at which Anne conceived by the king for the final time. At this point Jane Seymour probably wasn't even considered as anything more than a passing fancy. Once she realised that she was pregnant, Anne must also have known that her life depended not merely on carrying this child to full-term, but banking on the fact that it would be a boy.

It is entirely possible that a cause *besides* the terrible toll of patriarchal Tudor stress may have had a part to play in making sure that, after the birth of Elizabeth, Anne Boleyn was unable to carry another child to full term. Several writers and historians have speculated that she may have suffered from a disorder that meant that her body simply rejected the newly formed foetus after it had developed to a stage of several months, something that would only occur after a successful first birth but which would then go on to blight the chances of her ever carrying to full-term again. It seems that it was either this, or simply the aforementioned stress that struck Anne Boleyn time and time again and eventually helped bring about her downfall. Of course, given the fact that Catherine of Aragon also saw countless losses when it came to the bearing of children, it may have been something awry with the royal sperm that was to blame. It seems likely that we shall never know for sure. A great many historians have cast aspersions on the matter of the king's virility, and it became a subject of potential public ridicule when conversations between Anne and her brother George were repeated during the course of their trials, wherein it was said that Henry had neither virility nor the skill required to properly satisfy a woman.

Chapter 8

Cutting up the Carthusian Monks: The Terrible Death of a Tudor Traitor

Like Thomas More and Bishop Fisher, the Carthusian monks of the London Charterhouse at Smithfield were opposed to Henry VIII's decision to break with Rome, spurred on by the recalcitrance shown by the Pope in granting Henry a divorce from Catherine of Aragon so that he might marry Anne Boleyn. Like More and Fisher, the monks of the London Charterhouse would therefore also have to be destroyed, unless they could be made to bend to the king's will: 'When asked at their trial who they thought agreed with their opposition to the King's religious policy they had replied "All good men!"' (Lacey 1972, p143). And so it was that the first group of monks were sent to their deaths in May 1535, taken to the place of execution at Tyburn, near the present-day site of Marble Arch in London. This was the traditional location where traitors from the lower classes were executed in Tudor times. Nobles tended to be beheaded on Tower Hill, and if you were royalty, or perhaps just a really favoured courtier, you would be executed within the precincts of the Tower of London itself, on Tower Green. But it was at Tyburn that the Carthusian monks were to suffer the full horrors of a traitor's death, which meant that they were to be hung, drawn and quartered for the benefit of an often baying crowd.

The hanging came first. The monks were strung up in a row on large gallows which was then kicked out from beneath them and they were left suspended in mid-air almost until they lost consciousness. Once strung-up and suspended in such a fashion, they would writhe and kick their legs, wriggling from side to side, much to the amusement of the gathered crowds. They were then cut down before they were completely dead. It was of paramount importance, therefore, that the executioner keep an eye on each and every one of his charges so that they didn't 'accidentally' strangle while they were performing for their 'audience'.

25

Sometimes, after being cut down, they were given a moment to recover, or had water tossed in their faces in order to bring them around fully, the better to experience the second stage of the ordeal. However, if the executioner had received orders that he was to be particularly merciful then a victim would in fact be allowed to be hung until he was dead, even if his body were still to be quartered afterwards. It was not unheard of for an executioner to be paid by a member of the guilty party's family to allow them to strangle, although this was entirely at the executioner's discretion and of course went against the express wishes of the monarch.

The entirety of this process of execution would be witnessed by the public, and such an extensive execution as that of the Carthusians would have proven a considerable draw. Mass executions meant a whole day out for all the family, and people would arrive early or even sleep out overnight in order to get the best positions. There would be stalls set up selling fruit and drinks, and shortly afterwards pamphlets would circulate that would recall the whole thing in every glorious, gory detail. Not only were children not to be shielded from such a sight, but they were in fact positively encouraged to watch, the better to inculcate in them the idea that you disobeyed the monarch at your peril. Given the religious and political nature of many an execution, it seems also certain that there may have been some dissenters in the crowd as well. In 1535, when the Carthusians were despatched, England was still convulsing between Rome and the rule of Henry Tudor, and public opinion may well have lain far more firmly with the men than in the case of a simple traitor to the Crown.

Next in the general procedure of the execution, following on from the 'faux' hanging, the private parts of the monks would be cut off. This was done in such a way – the exact method is not known, be it dagger or sword – so that the victim did not bleed to death before being forced to endure the third stage of the ordeal, namely the dreaded disembowelling. Quite possibly the castration wound was quickly cauterised in order to prevent blood loss, which might otherwise have deprived the crowd of their next portion of 'fun'. When the monks – or indeed anyone suffering the traitor's death – were finally disembowelled, their stomach was sliced open – sometimes with a hot blade, sometimes with a cool one – and then their intestines were either scooped out by the executioner's bare hands, or, if he had been ordered to make more of a show of it, thus further prolonging the agony, he might curl the intestines around on a rolling pin and draw them out that way, in other words really, *really* slowly. The intestines were then tossed onto a nearby fire where the genitals of the victim were already being flame-grilled. The monks certainly would have been encouraged to bear witness to the sight of their innards being consumed by the flames. Death was swift from this point onward, but they would still have been alive by the time they were dragged to the executioner's block itself, by which time beheading them would almost have been a mercy. Being able to perform a good hanging, drawing, and quartering was seen to be a considerable art on the part of an executioner, given that it was greatly desired that the victim should not die before the full rigours of the punishment had been served.

Lastly, the dead bodies of the monks would have been quartered, which basically meant that they were hacked into four vaguely symmetrical parts – arms and legs and head and torso – and the various offending pieces would then be stuck up at the various city gates of London – sometimes they were distributed around the country if a wider warning of the pitfalls of treason was required – or on the spikes normally used for such a purpose at London Bridge. Thomas More's head was impaled on just such a pole on London Bridge until his daughter Margaret snuck out one night and retrieved it. More was lucky in that he had been spared the full horrors of a traitor's death. Others among the Carthusian monks were also fortunate in that they starved to death in prison before being given over to the executioner – either by design or simply because they were forgotten – and thus before they could suffer the same fate as their compatriots.

The actual punishment of hanging, drawing and quartering was not in fact abolished until well into the reign of Queen Victoria, in 1870. Astonishingly, beheading, for the crime of treason, was not abolished until 1973, although the last person actually to be beheaded in England was way back in 1747. For those with a rather morbid sense of humour, the Hung Drawn & Quartered pub on Great Tower Street in the City of London is only a stone's throw from the site of execution on Tower Hill, where Thomas More and countless others lost their lives during the reign of Henry VIII.

Chapter 9

The Blackened Heart of Catherine of Aragon: Cancer in Tudor Times

Catherine of Aragon died on 7 January 1536, at the age of fifty. Having been abandoned by Henry VIII in favour of Anne Boleyn, she had been exiled to a series of increasingly draughty castles in the Midlands, culminating in a tenure of some several months in her final destination of Kimbolton Castle in Cambridgeshire. She never gave up her love for her husband, nor, one suspects, the faintest of hopes that he might one day come to his senses and restore her to the position from which she had been so unjustly gouged. It was from Kimbolton Castle that she wrote her final touching letter to the man who had so callously cast her aside, knowing in her diseased heart that she did not have long left to live:

My most dear lord, King and husband,

The hour of my death now drawing on, the tender love I ouge [owe] thou forceth me, my case being such, to commend myselv to thou, and to put thou in remembrance with a few words of the healthe and safeguard of thine allm [soul] which thou ougte to preferce before all worldley matters, and before the care and pampering of thy body, for the which thoust have cast me into many calamities and thineselv into many troubles. For my part, I pardon thou everything, and I desire to devoutly pray God that He will pardon thou also. For the rest, I commend unto thou our doughtere Mary, beseeching thou to be a good father unto her, as I have heretofore desired. I entreat thou also, on behalve of my maides, to give them marriage portions, which is not much, they being but three. For all mine other servants I solicit the wages due them, and a year more, lest they be unprovided for. Lastly, I makest this vouge (vow), that mine eyes desire thou aboufe all things.

Katharine the Queen.

After her death, her body was duly embalmed and it was then that there was found to be a 'monstrous' black growth about her heart, or possibly even that her entire heart had in fact turned black and warped. This led some at the court to speculate that she had been poisoned, probably by Anne Boleyn. Given the rumours had that had circulated during the poisoning of Bishop Fisher, it is not impossible to see how some people came to this conclusion, especially if they were partisans of Catherine. Modern science has since stepped in and attributed the blackening of Catherine's heart to be due most likely to a more recognizable malady, i.e., cancer. Or perhaps she quite simply died of a broken heart; grief and shame at her loss of both husband and status may have not merely incubated her illness but also quite possibly accelerated it as well.

Henry's reaction to his wife's death was a show of great jubilation, even more so for Anne Boleyn: 'He and Anne showed great joy and appear to have celebrated the occasion. Anne gave a "handsome present" to the messenger who brought her news of Catherine's death' (Lipscomb, 2009, p52). Henry and Anne were also seen sporting bright yellow colours, although these were in fact the traditional colours of mourning in Spain. Whether this was a genuine tribute or instead a display of malicious irony is something that shall perhaps never be known, but certainly they were in fine spirits at the time, with Henry showing his daughter Elizabeth off to all the court while a proud Anne Boleyn looked on. In Anne's mind it must have then seemed as though Catherine's death had confirmed the fact that she was now the one true queen of England, but it actually left her in a desperately vulnerable position. As far as Europe was concerned – and it was still almost entirely Catholic at this time – Anne was a usurper and her marriage to Henry was laughably invalid. In the king's eyes, with Catherine dead he was now therefore a widower and free to marry once again.

Chapter 10

A Shapeless Mass of Flesh: Anne Boleyn's Lost Prince

Anne Boleyn's final miscarriage occurred on 29 January 1536. A range of historical speculators have said that it was in response to hearing that the king had fallen from his horse and been crushed during a jousting accident, while others said that she had come upon the king with Jane Seymour sitting on his knee, demurely whispering sweet nothings in his ear. Perhaps it was a combination of the two, and perhaps neither. As detailed in previous chapters, it may have been simply that Anne suffered from a disorder that meant she could not carry any child after her first one to full term. Whatever the ultimate cause, it was clear that the queen had 'miscarried of her saviour'. The baby boy would have been the perfect bargaining chip by which to best the might of patriarchy, but tragically for Anne it was not to be.

On hearing of the loss, Henry would shortly come to the conclusion that God would allow him no male children by Anne Boleyn, and therefore in order to sire a legitimate male heir he would need to remarry again, post-haste. Worse still, it was then reported second-hand that he had been heard uttering that he had 'been seduced into this marriage by witchcraft'. By a chilling coincidence, which few have failed to leave unmolested, 29 January was also the day that Catherine of Aragon was laid to rest in Peterborough Cathedral. Her partisans – and many modern authors – have long spun a poetic line about her chilly fingers reaching out from the grave in order to tickle free the child from Anne's womb.

Although Anne Boleyn was never actually charged with witchcraft, the belief in such things was widespread at the time: 'Witches also allegedly engaged in illicit sexual intercourse, for they reportedly committed a number of sexual acts that their contemporaries viewed as deviant. Although experts continued to argue about whether the union between witches and the devil, called sodomy, could result in normal childbirth, they agreed that witches gave birth to deformed children, made demonic sacrifices of infants, including their own offspring, and committed incest' (Warnicke, 1989, p192). In fact, such was the prevalence of thought regarding witchcraft at the time that common gossip most likely became garbled with the actual accusations that were eventually levelled at Anne Boleyn during her trial. The Tudor mind was that most bizarre hybrid of the medieval and the Renaissance, in that it could juggle the concepts of taxes and loans and also witches and demons in the same thought process and yet still come up with an utterly logical – to them, at least – and viable answer to the problem of both in one lucid sentence.

Suspected witches were often judged on their affinity with the supernatural by being sewn into a sack and then tossed into the nearest ample body of water. If they survived this attempted drowning then they were a witch and were thus summarily executed, but if they drowned then they were innocent of all wrongdoing; again, a classic example of the bizarre hybrid of the medieval and the Renaissance mind. Another slightly less lethal manner of discerning the identity of a witch was to have them recite the Lord's Prayer without making a single mistake. The tongue of a witch was thought to be so treacherous that it was deemed impossible that they could utter something so holy without choking on the sheer goodness of the words. It wasn't until 1542, some six years or so after the execution of Anne Boleyn, that Parliament passed the Witchcraft Act. Practising witchcraft was thus decreed an offence punishable by death, although the act was then repealed five years later, before being reinstated in a somewhat modified form in 1562.

Alongside the belief in witchcraft, Tudor society as a whole was intensely – one might almost say pathologically – superstitious, thus explaining why Henry VIII might have possibly uttered with a straight face the idea that he had been seduced into his marriage with Anne Boleyn by means of sorcery. For one thing, with such a high mortality rate, Tudor society often took measures into their own hands when it came to warding off the icy fingers of the grim reaper. For instance, where the safety of a newborn was concerned, church bells might be rung in order to ward away any marauding evil spirits. By the same token, it was said to be unlucky to swaddle a newborn in new clothing, and so for the first several hours of its life any baby might instead find itself wrapped up in some stale old length of cloth, until the immediate vicinity might be deemed safe from rampaging sprites. It was also said to be extremely unlucky for a hare to run across your path, because hares were apparently one of the myriad shapes that witches used to sprint around the country. In the centuries following her death, the legend of a hare in the vicinity of Blickling Hall in Norfolk, birthplace of Anne Boleyn, has become cemented in local lore.

In the centuries following Anne Boleyn's final miscarriage, it has become part of the popular legends surrounding her that the child she lost was 'a shapeless mass of flesh', or in some way hideously deformed, with a spine bursting out of its back, or failing that then perhaps looking like something spewed up by Satan himself. The one 'viable' source for this slander is the Catholic propagandist Nicholas Sanders, writing his twisted take on things well after the event. This was the same Nicholas Sanders who also said that Anne had six fingers, that her body was covered in moles – 'the devil's teats' – and that she had a huge growth under her chin – sometimes called a 'wen' – that she hid with high collars. All of these 'deformities' went quite unremarked upon at the time she was alive by any observers, hostile or otherwise.

The six finger rumour in particular has become so strong and so embedded in English folklore that for most people it is the starting point of any conversation concerning Anne Boleyn, alongside 'So did she really have it away with her brother?' As for Nicholas Sanders himself, he was born in Surrey in or around 1530, meaning that he was still just a small child when Anne Boleyn suffered her final miscarriage. As an adult he went to Rome, where he eventually became a priest, producing several works on the trials of English Catholics. It was these works that eventually led him to write the specific slanders against Anne Boleyn, who was at that point viewed by many in the Catholic Church as being one of the main proponents of the heretical Protestant faith. No matter how far removed we may be from these original events, it seems unlikely that these slanders against Anne Boleyn will ever be quite forgotten. Indeed, to her supporters they serve to illustrate the lengths to she was attacked (in Spain one of the terms of opprobrium for an adulterous woman is apparently a play on her name). Several centuries down the line Anne Boleyn remains as divisive a topic dead as she ever did when she was alive.

The accusations of incest that were eventually levelled at Anne Boleyn during her arrest and trial led some commentators to speculate –

retrospectively, for the most part – that the aborted foetus may have been deformed because it was the result of some sort of an illicit liaison with her brother George. Incestuous liaisons were in Tudor times considered to bring forth hideous monstrosities, and several of the royal houses of Europe were known for their inbreeding, particularly the Hapsburgs and their famous 'Hapsburg lip'. Henry VIII and his third wife, Jane Seymour, were in fact fifth cousins, though the distance was considered suitable enough to avoid any particular problems. Egyptians believed that the royal women carried the bloodlines and therefore it was considered wise for a pharaoh to marry his sister, thus doubling up the sacred genes. Whether these births turned out quite as planned is unclear.

In Tudor times witches were thought to give birth to deformed children, and here these two trains of Tudor tittle-tattle may have become tangled in the popular imagination of the time, before then being generously frothed up by the lies of Nicholas Sanders. Historians such as G.W. Bernard, as well as the popular novelist Philippa Gregory, have speculated that Anne Boleyn *did* in fact sleep with her brother George, but that it was a contrived and desperate act between the two siblings to get her pregnant and ensure both hers and her family's survival in the face of Henry VIII's lack of prowess, as well as his increasing lack of ardour where his queen was concerned. At her trial, it was said that Anne Boleyn was so insatiable that she had slept with her brother simply to satisfy her own rampant desires, 'drinking the pot to its very dregs', but not even her enemies, the ambassador Chapuys among them, were really convinced by these garish tales of her guilt. Given the fact that she faced certain ruin unless she produced a male heir – and given that Henry was fast losing faith in her – it is not outside of the realms of possibility that Anne and her brother may have resorted to this last, desperate roll of the dice. Their names will remain forever linked because of this one insalubrious fact, but if you were to imagine yourself in their place, with Jane Seymour lurking on the periphery … well, desperate times require desperate measures. To even consider it takes no lustre from Anne Boleyn's legend, but in fact merely serves to more greatly illuminate her tragedy.

Chapter 11

'She Has Had to Do With Over a Hundred Men!' Anne Boleyn and the Tudor Take on Female Promiscuity

Anne Boleyn was arrested on 2 May 1536 at Greenwich Palace and taken by barge to the Tower of London. Her brother George was arrested soon after, accused – among other things – of the astonishing crime of incest with his sister. Also taken, before and after them, were the queen's young musician, Mark Smeaton, as well as Henry Norris, who was one of Henry VIII's closet companions, William Brereton, a groom of the king's chamber, and the young courtier Francis Weston. In the days that followed, the poet Thomas Wyatt was also arrested, as was Sir Richard Page, another courtier. These two would later be released without charge.

Anne Boleyn's history with Thomas Wyatt stretched back to way before her marriage to Henry Tudor, but the precise details remain, as always, elusive. Either way, all of these men were accused of having had sexual relations with the queen on various unverifiable dates and at locations too numerous and widespread to be taken at all seriously, although the court that tried the queen did just that. Anne Boleyn and her harem of lovers were also accused of plotting the death of the king, of laughing at his dress sense – or the lack of it – and also his lack of musical accomplishment, as well as publicly deriding the much-vaunted royal virility. As the rumours flew and the arrests continued, the monstrous reputation of Anne Boleyn as a man-eating necromancer really began to take shape in the popular imagination.

The king himself came to believe in due course that she had in fact had at least a hundred lovers, if not more. He even took to writing a play or a series of short verses about the fact that he was now a monumental cuckold, which he carried about with him and tried to show to various embarrassed friends and courtiers at any given moment. The king seemed to have no shame at all in being seen as a cuckold, a situation that has

34

led some historians to speculate whether or not there was some truth to the charges (else why risk the reputation of such an overly masculine monarch?). Others have suggested that the accusations against Anne Boleyn were framed to be so monstrous that it appeared that no man alive could possibly have sated her rampant desires, and that this is why the charge of incest with her brother George was included amongst them. However, at present it seems that most historians believe that Anne Boleyn *was* framed in regard to her infidelities, with the notable exception of G.W. Bernard, who is aided in his opinions by the undeniable fact that some of the trial papers are lost, and that these 'killer documents' may hold vital evidence that could swing the pendulum more decisively in the direction of her guilt, or simply magnify to an even greater extent what a tissue of lies the whole torrid affair was.

The accused men – George Boleyn aside – were all tried in Westminster Hall and all were found guilty of adultery with the queen. The head of the guard's axe, which would have been turned away from them on their entrance, was turned so that the blade was facing towards them as they were escorted out, signifying both their guilt and their imminent death. Anne Boleyn and her brother were tried separately from the others because they were nobles, on 15 May 1536, in a part of the Tower of London that no longer exists. Anne conducted herself gallantly and with considerable aplomb, by all accounts. At one point she even admitted that she had not always shown her husband the respect and deference which were his due, but this was in no way an admission of adultery on her part. However, the weight of popular opinion was against her, and she was found guilty and condemned to be either burned or beheaded, according to the king's pleasure. 'Anne listened with the same dignified composure she had maintained throughout the trial. She regretted only that innocent men must die with her, and that she had not always "borne toward the king the humility which I owed him." That was as close to a sneer as she could allow herself' (Lindsey, 1995, p127).

Anne's brother fared so well in his trial that bets were placed that he might even be acquitted at the very last moment, but he then committed legal – and social – suicide by reading out in court a document that declared Henry VIII to be a sexually impotent fool, evidence apparently supplied from the tongue of his wife, the 'infamous' Lady Rochford. After that, his fate, like that of his sister, was swiftly sealed. All of the men – George Boleyn included – were beheaded on Tower Hill on

17 May, with only Mark Smeaton the musician maintaining his guilt right up until the very end. Pleas for clemency from various family members had all fallen on deaf ears in the days leading up to the executions. Their decapitated bodies were tossed into a kind of mass grave that surrounds the chapel of St Peter ad Vincula, inside the precincts of the Tower of London, where they remain to this day, along with countless other traitors to the Tudor throne.

As regards Anne Boleyn's sexual proclivities, a modern audience will see this for the blatant exercise in 'slut-shaming' that it undoubtedly was. That Anne may have flirted and bantered with these men is quite possible, but in Tudor times there was but a small stretch between flirtation and fornication, especially where a woman was concerned. It was the eternal dichotomy of 'the virgin and the whore', and a woman was to be expected to be the former and roundly condemned if her behaviour was somehow seen as her leaning somewhat towards the latter. The fact was that Anne had played Henry like a harp, seducing him and then holding him at arm's length, and the wrecking of her reputation may have been a game of Chinese whispers that originated with the king himself, or perhaps from a source quite close to the king. The more unpalatable a woman's reputation, the more likely the public were to swallow the charge that she was some sort of nymph.

Chapter 12

The Racking of Mark Smeaton

The Flemish musician Mark Smeaton was a member of Cardinal Wolsey's household before the premier prelate's spectacular fall from grace, and from there Smeaton eventually ended up in Anne Boleyn's entourage. Once firmly ensconced within the confines of the court, Smeaton was apparently seen as something of a social climber, but was on one occasion quickly put in his place by the queen, who told him that she would not speak to him 'as if he were a gentleman because he was only a man of inferior birth and status'. Smeaton replied rather salaciously that a look from the queen was enough for him to be getting on with, but somehow various details of the otherwise discreet conversation worked their way back to Thomas Cromwell, who was at the time busying himself with bringing about Anne Boleyn's downfall, spying an ideal opportunity to turn a chance exchange into something far more sinister. A similarly indiscreet exchange between the queen and Sir Henry Norris, whereby Anne told him that 'were anything to happen to the king then he would look to have her', had the unfortunate effect of making sure that Norris, a close friend of the king, joined the men who were to soon be accused of adultery with the doomed queen. In Smeaton's case, as Antonia Fraser put it, 'so the handsome young musician Mark Smeaton was accused of being in love with the Queen as well as receiving money from her. His fine clothes had aroused jealousy, considering his poor background and slender allowance from the King' (Fraser, 1993, p306). The truth or otherwise of these allegations will probably never be known, as will the real reasons why this poor young wretch cleaved to the queen in such an indiscreet manner.

Mark Smeaton was arrested or 'taken' on 30 April 1536 to Thomas Cromwell's house at Stepney, where he confessed, under torture, to adultery with the queen. Apparently a knotted length of cord was tied around his head, with the pressure slowly applied by twisting the cloth at one end so that one of the knots might then gouge his eye out. In her novel *Bring up the Bodies* Hilary Mantel maintains that this was a piece of fiction, and that Smeaton was actually just verbally intimidated by the various members of Cromwell's household instead – the same goes for the TV adaptation – but one must bear in mind that Cromwell was Mantel's 'fictional' hero, and she may have been loath to have him doing anything *too* reprehensible. Either way, the following day Smeaton was taken to the Tower of London and supposedly put on the rack – some have cited this as another exaggeration for which there is little proof – but at this point he did confess for a second time and admitted adultery with the queen, also naming several other members of her household. It was this confession that helped in part to secure the arrests of the other men, including the queen's own brother. Needless to say, any confession extracted under torture is hardly worth the paper it's written on, but this plain piece of logic seems not to have troubled the Tudor regime at all. Henry VIII and Anne Boleyn were attending the May Day jousts when news of Smeaton's confession was brought to the king, causing him to depart in a hurry, and taking Henry Norris with him. Norris was accused by the king on the ride back to London from Greenwich, and promptly placed in the Tower. Anne Boleyn never saw her husband again.

The rack – an archival example of which still exists at the Tower of London, for the morbidly-minded – was a wooden frame raised up from the ground, long enough for a man to be fully laid out on, with rollers positioned at either end and one in the middle, this one equipped with a row of iron teeth. The prisoner was tied to the rollers by the wrists at one end and by the ankles at the other, and then the handle and ratchet mechanism were turned so that the victim was first lifted up off the wooden frame and then slowly stretched taut, to the point where they would be suspended almost in mid-air above the wooden frame. Any further turning of the handle – and subsequent operation of the ratchet mechanism – would mean that the slow dislocation of various joints would soon follow, with the accompanying muscles being stretched and then also torn in the process. In this way, feet might be dislocated from legs, even as knee joints were plucked free from the upper leg, and hips were divided downwards, while the spine was eased to a length whereupon it might snap, like a length of elastic. Often, for those observing, this torture would be accompanied by the sounds of the various bones and ligaments popping out of place. The pain was, of course, excruciating, and as a result the rack was so feared that the mere sight of it could cause a man to confess his guilt, or even to confess to something he wasn't actually guilty of in the first place, simply in order to be taken back to his cell. Sometimes prisoners were simply 'lightly' racked, i.e., scant use of the mechanism was employed, and this may have been enough to induce a 'confession' without causing any lasting bodily damage. This method was sometimes referred to as 'pinching', which 'could mean a range of physical discomfort from irritation and annoyance to torture and torment.' (Alford, 2013, p163).

For those who think that women generally had it far worse in Tudor times, it is worth noting that only men were allowed to be racked, the one deviation from the usage of this dreaded device being the case of Anne Askew, the Protestant preacher, in 1546. She had to be carried to the stake where she was to be burnt on a chair after suffering an illegal session on the rack. There are differing records as to whether Mark Smeaton was equally injured when he came to be beheaded on Tower Hill on the 17 May 1536. As a 'mercy', Anne Askew was *apparently* allowed a small bag of gunpowder secreted about her person as she was lashed to the stake, which ignited as the first few flames lapped at it, thus sparing her the further agony of the fire. Several others suffering with her were thus also mercifully despatched. If gunpowder were not available, then, at the executioner's discretion, victims due to be burned might be lashed to the stake in such a way that they actually strangled before they were consumed by the flames.

The injuries caused by the rack were exacerbated by the generally harsh conditions in which many of these victims – Mark Smeaton included, if indeed he was racked – were subjected to after they had been tortured. They would have been returned to their cells with all of their various limbs and ligaments torn out of place, without any resort to pain relief, to pass who knew how many days and nights before finally being put out of their misery. It seems a wonder that any of them were left alive to be hauled before the axe or else cast into the fire, but survive they did. Unfortunately for those poor denizens of the Tower of London, the human body could be remarkably resilient, even under the most awful forms of duress.

Aside from the rack, there were plenty of other instruments of torture available for interrogating prisoners at the Tower of London. One such instrument was the 'Scavenger's Daughter', the invention of Sir Leonard Skevington, who was Lieutenant of the Tower in the reign of

Henry VIII. This was a charming device which looked rather like a giant upright compass. It was in fact an A-frame rack shape, one which 'held the neck, wrists and ankles in a linked restraint' (Haynes 2004, p58). The head of the victim was secured at the very pinnacle, with the arms and legs at the lower points of the 'A'. The frame could then be folded, thus contorting the body into an unnatural sitting position, compressing organs and joints together and causing considerable internal damage. Another much-favoured device were the manacles, whereby prisoners might be suspended by the wrists and then left to dangle just above the floor, with the subsequent strain leaving their hands and fingers permanently damaged. The Jesuit priest John Gerard, apprehended in 1594, gave blunt testimony to the pain that the manacles could cause: 'such a gripping pain came over me. It was worst in my chest and belly, my hands and arms. All the blood in my body seemed to rush up into my arms and hands and I thought that blood was oozing out from the ends of my fingers; the pain was so intense that I thought I could not possibly endure it' (Plowden, 2010, p218).

Sleep deprivation was often used as a more subtle means of coercing information out of a prisoner, as in the case of Anthony Babington (more of whom later) when he was captured after masterminding a plot to have Elizabeth I assassinated, and Mary Queen of Scots placed on the English throne in her place. Subtler still, sometimes prisoners were simply placed in cells that were directly within earshot of the various torture chambers, as an incentive to confess before more stringent measures were employed. To this end, multiple plotters might be placed strategically in chambers adjoining the torture chamber and thus forced to listen to the cries of their compatriots. Some prison cells were designed to torment the occupant by proximity to either the dampness of the river or from the very extremities of the elements themselves. One cell in particular was notorious for the very particular discomfort it could cause. Nicknamed 'Little Ease', this tiny space was located beneath the Tower of London's White Tower. The measurements were so limited that the occupant could neither stand, sit nor lie down. The Catholic priest Edmund Campion is said to have spent some time in 'Little Ease' during the reign of Elizabeth I.

Even after Mark Smeaton's death there were those who believed that Elizabeth Tudor was in fact his illegitimate child. A particular proponent of this rather laughable rumour (no one who saw Elizabeth believed that she was anyone but Henry VIII's red-haired, bad-tempered little girl) was Elizabeth's half-sister Mary, who no doubt would have delighted in the discredit such a rumour would have brought to her popular sibling had it turned out to be true. Despite the accusation of incest, the rumour that Elizabeth might possibly have been her uncle George Boleyn's daughter was far less widespread, as was the idea that Elizabeth might also be the child of Henry Norris, or indeed one of the others thus accused. Because of the fact of his 'low birth', almost any modern movie or TV drama concerning the downfall of Anne Boleyn will have a version of Mark Smeaton thrown in there somewhere, purely for the class contrast, whereas her other 'lovers' are often cherry-picked according to casting constraints. (Mark Smeaton stood out amongst Anne Boleyn's alleged lovers because he was a commoner, whereas the others, all noblemen of varying degrees, are often used or disregarded in the various adaptations accordingly.)

Chapter 13

Anne Boleyn and the Swordsman of Calais

Anne Boleyn was executed on 19 May 1536, in the grounds of the Tower of London. This pivotal moment in history took place directly between the White Tower and the Waterloo Block, the latter being the location where the crown jewels are currently housed. She was most certainly *not* executed on the site of the glass memorial to those beheaded within the walls of the Tower, despite what the Beefeaters and several less well-informed books about Anne Boleyn might try to tell you. The actual, authentic spot of her execution isn't marked, but if you station yourself directly between the White Tower and the Waterloo Block then you're probably in pretty much the right position. If you visit the Tower of London on the date of her execution then you're sure to see a great many of her fans coming to pay tribute, with flowers being left either on the aforementioned glass memorial or else in the chapel of St Peter ad Vincula itself.

Rather than subject his second wife to the blunt humiliation and the often botched brutality of the axe – death by burning had also been mooted at one point during her trial – Henry VIII showed his disgraced queen a special 'mercy' by farming out the task to the famed swordsman of Calais. He would execute her in the more merciful French fashion, with a far sharper, more agile blade rather than a clumsy axe. Execution in the French fashion involved the prisoner kneeling rather than being sprawled out in an ungainly manner over a bloodstained block of wood, and the actual beheading itself was usually achieved in one swift stroke, rather than the ungainly hacking that sometimes accompanied an execution by axe. The swordsman had actually been sent for several days ahead of the outcome of Anne's trial, so her 'guilt' was never in any doubt, although his delay in arriving – problems with horseshoes – meant that there were several unintentionally sadistic false-starts to Anne's perceived final days. She mentally prepared herself for execution on several occasions only to be told that her imminent death had in fact been delayed because the swordsman, who might be swift when it came to lopping off heads, was in terms of timekeeping something of a slacker.

The swordsman of Calais's special, 'civilised' method of execution also involved wearing a pair of soft-soled shoes as he scampered about the scaffold, so as not to alarm his victim. He would then distract his victims by calling out for his sword to his young boy assistant, who would be standing nearby. In fact, the sword would have been secreted elsewhere and the swordsman would pick it up as his victim turned their head to follow the sound of his request. At that precise moment, the swordsman would strike, the sinews on the neck of the victim being exposed to the maximum effect when the head was turned in such a way. Anne Boleyn was executed in exactly this manner, and her head was taken off so swiftly and so cleanly that many of the spectators for several seconds afterwards doubted what they had actually witnessed. Her lips were said to move for a further several minutes afterwards while her ladies were busily bundling her body into a nearby arrow-chest. No provision had been made for her disgraced corpse following her death, unbelievably, although whether this was an intentional slight or simply a gruesome oversight has never been adequately explained.

The graphic reality of execution by beheading was brought starkly to light by the famed historian Alison Weir, in the closing pages of her book *The Lady in the Tower*. She cites the work of several French doctors whose experiments in the realm of death by decapitation concluded that almost every element of brain and body survives decapitation, however briefly, and that consciousness was indeed possible for the victim for several minutes afterwards. It is described by them as 'a savage vivisection': 'In 1983, another medical study found that "no matter how efficient the method of execution, at least two to three seconds of intense pain cannot be avoided"' (Weir, 2009, p272). This leads to the dreadful thought that the victims of beheadings may have been aware and cognisant for a very brief time after their head was separated from the body. Indeed, when the head was held up by the executioner as proof of his success – as it often was – the victim may have still been 'alive' and thus staring out at the astonished crowd.

Before Anne Boleyn was subjected to this 'savage vivisection', she gave a short but eloquent speech to the assembled onlookers, telling them, among other things, that Henry VIII was the most kind and loving prince a wife and a kingdom could ever hope to have had. It simply wasn't good form to bad-mouth one's ex-husband on the scaffold when that ex-husband happened to be the king and when the fate of your daughter and also the rest of your family needed to be considered:

> Good Christian people, I have not come here to preach a sermon; I have come here to die, for according to the law and by the law I am judged to die, and thereof I will speak nothing against it. I am come hither to accuse no man, nor to speak of that whereof I am accused and condemned to die, but I pray God save the King and send him long to reign over you, for a gentler nor a more merciful prince was there never, and to me he was ever a good, a gentle, and sovereign lord.
>
> And if any person will meddle of my cause, I require them to judge the best. And thus I take my leave of the world and of you all, and I heartily desire you all to pray for me.

She was calm and composed throughout, but once her words were done and she was kneeling and awaiting the blindfold, she apparently kept glancing over her shoulder at the swordsman, her prayers half muttered. Quite possibly the blindfold was administered in order to prevent a post-decapitation view on the part of the condemned, or to save them from the curious faces of the crowd. It cannot have been to spare them the sight of the weapon itself, because the blow would always fall from behind or to the far side of their body. The pain would have been intense when the blow fell, but mercifully brief. She may have survived decapitation by several seconds or even by a minute or more, but equally, it may be that the shock of the blow killed her outright.

The swordsman of Calais was paid £23 6s 8d for his services. His real name is unknown, nor is it certain that he even originated from Calais. The identities of executioners were often kept a secret, for fear of retribution on the part of the families of their victims. Therefore, whatever happened to the actual sword that decapitated Anne Boleyn also remains a mystery. Were such a relic ever to be discovered then it would doubtless be considered quite priceless, though the provenance would be exceedingly difficult to prove. Whoever he was, the swordsman of Calais went to his grave without ever apparently disclosing how he felt about performing one of the most famous beheadings in human history. Even at the time, the execution of Anne Boleyn was quite astonishing – she was the first queen of England ever to suffer such a fate – and he can have been in little doubt that he had secured his own particular place in history for having performed such an act.

Chapter 14

Putting Out the Pilgrimage of Grace

The Pilgrimage of Grace – a large-scale uprising/rebellion – was the biggest single threat to Henry VIII's throne and to the Tudor regime as a whole. It came about as a direct result of the king's new religious policy, and most importantly because of the fact that Thomas Cromwell was dissolving the monasteries around the country quicker than a couple of soluble aspirins in a Tudor tankard. There was most definitely a 'north-south' aspect to the incident, typified by the fact that the seat of power was in London, which, in 1536, was considerably further from the north than it is today, certainly in terms of travel time. All in all, the uprising lasted a little over a year, and would be the largest rebellion that Henry VIII would face.

The Pilgrimage of Grace fomented in Yorkshire from October 1536 onwards, and such was the ardour and the mood of the masses that it soon spread to the surrounding areas; a smaller uprising had in fact occurred in Lincolnshire some twelve days earlier to the main rebellion. The London barrister Robert Aske – 'Mr Aske' – was appointed as the leader of the uprising, alongside Baron Darcy and a member of the Tudor gentry called Robert Constable. Under Mr Aske's leadership, the rebels rapidly occupied York, marching under a collection of banners that depicted the wounds of Christ, effectively setting out their Catholic credentials in opposition to the fact that Henry VIII had effectively removed England from the papal yoke.

As a result of this effort, the rebels effectively restored Catholicism in the city, and several of Henry's nobles were forced to treat with them rather than resort to warfare and brute force because of the sheer numbers and effectiveness of the enemy. Given sure promises of a royal pardon from the king, the rebels of the Pilgrimage of Grace were convinced that it was safe to disband their demonstration, and so the rebellion at this point effectively dispersed itself. Mr Aske even travelled to London to meet the king, where he received further assurances of a royal pardon and at least partial acquiescence to the demands his rebels were making. Henry also presented him with a nice new coat as proof of his credentials, although, given future form, it seems almost certain that Henry was dissembling.

However, renewed rebellions broke out in the north – at East Riding in Yorkshire – without Mr Aske's permission and this gave Henry VIII the opportunity to renege on all of his promises. Mr Aske and the other leaders were promptly arrested and Aske was brutally hanged in chains in York, outside Clifford's Tower, all that remains of the now-ruined York Castle. Baron Darcy was beheaded on Tower Hill, while Robert Constable was hanged in Hull. As far as the followers of the rebellion were concerned, the reprisals were savage: 'Henry used this as an excuse to arrest and execute nearly all the leaders of the earlier revolt and to hang some four hundred of their followers, not for their participation in the first rebellion, for which they had been pardoned, but on trumped-up charges of having taken part in the second abortive rising' (Ridley, 2002, p233). Queen Jane Seymour – wife number three – had apparently begged the king to show some leniency to the rebels – she was said to have been 'of the Catholic persuasion' – but Henry was not in the mood to be merciful and told her not to meddle. In fact, he apparently went so far as to add the rather sinister caveat that becoming involved in matters of state was what had led to the execution of his previous wife. This was the closest perhaps that Henry ever got to actually admitting that Anne Boleyn had been set up, and that her execution had nothing whatsoever to do with a 'deformed foetus', or from having illicit relations with her brother. A clash with Cromwell over policy may have had far more to do with it.

Chapter 15

The Death of Jane Seymour: Childbirth in Tudor Times

On 12 October 1537, in a small room in Hampton Court Palace, now used mainly for paid costumed performers to change their clothes, Henry VIII's third wife, Jane Seymour, gave birth to his much longed-for legitimate male heir. The labour was protracted, overly painful, and in the end lasted for almost three whole days. It is quite possible that the baby was in a bad position – breech perhaps – and it has been further speculated that the midwives attending on the queen simply did not have the knowledge necessary to turn the child correctly, thus allowing for a relatively smooth birth.

Prenatal care was, in some respects, shockingly primitive in Tudor times, and the mortality rate in childbirth was high. However, despite this, there were a great many women who gave birth to large numbers of children and survived. Jane's sister-in-law Anne Stanhope, the Duchess of Somerset and wife of Edward Seymour, gave birth to no fewer than ten children during the course of their marriage. Women who were due to give birth often made their wills, said farewell to friends and family and settled all of their worldly affairs before retiring to the privacy of the birthing chamber, or wherever it was that they would deliver their child.

It is possible – although unlikely – that in order to hasten the birth of Henry VIII's heir and relieve her suffering Jane Seymour may have had some sort of caesarean procedure performed on her, and the fourth episode of season three of *The Tudors* speculates on this scenario in highly dramatic style. However, this theory has been widely debunked by those who say that it was a myth started in Elizabethan times by Catholics propagandists who wanted to cite the deeply Protestant King Edward VI's birth as somehow 'unnatural'. The first modern caesarean section was not recorded as having been performed until 1881, but caesareans were, in fact, known in Tudor times, though they were almost always performed only in crisis, normally when the mother had already died during childbirth and there was still perceived hope of saving the baby. Any woman who was still alive when undergoing a caesarean section in Tudor times would almost certainly have died straight after the operation because of the lack of knowledge surrounding such a procedure, or because of the risk of infection afterwards.

As it turned out, Jane Seymour *did* die of some sort of infection following her extremely prolonged and traumatic labour, but this was a full twelve days after the fact of the birth. Most speculation seems to have settled on the idea that the infection came from a tear in her perineum. Therefore, this gap of twelve days seems almost too wide a window to allow the caesarean theory to really take hold, although accounts are still so conflicting that it cannot be ruled out completely. It is more than likely that the aforementioned tear in her perineum during the delivery then became infected and that she died as a result of the infection spreading. Either that or part of the placenta was retained in the womb and the midwives were possibly negligent in this regard. As previously stated, while many women during Tudor times died in childbirth, millions more did not, so practice and procedure may not have been as primitive as we might think.

Jane Seymour was understandably weak following the birth and never really regained her strength. Following a brief point at which she appeared to rally, there was a rapid weakening in her constitution a day or so before she died. This sudden weakening was followed by a violent 'listing' in her bowels and she then died on 24 October.

There was some generalised talk afterwards from various parties that she had died because of some neglect on the part of her midwives, and this does seem to suggest that mistakes were indeed made during the birth which should have been picked up on even by those *relatively* primitive standards of the time. The king himself wasn't with her when she died; he had 'removed' to Esher when it became clear that her condition was critical and that little or nothing could be done to save her. This can either be taken as a clear display of callousness on the part of the often ruthless Tudor tyrant, or as a sign of the fact that he was so distraught at what had befallen the wife who had given him a son that he simply could not face the fact that she was now on the verge of death. 'Henry, perhaps reasoning that there was nothing he could do for Jane, could no longer bear to remain nearby and determined to leave her, regardless of the events of the night' (Norton 2009, p147). Henry's mother, Elizabeth of York, had died after giving birth in 1503 to a baby girl who also died, and thus the entire scenario may simply have been too painful for the king to confront.

Certainly, Jane Seymour would have been prepared for the birth in the traditional Tudor style, which basically meant being holed up in a sunless room for four to six weeks ahead of the estimated arrival date. Sunlight and fresh air were thought to be damaging to the unborn child and also to the fragile constitution of the mother, and so the windows were kept shut in order to keep out any harmful vapours. Anne Boleyn also had to deal with this period of protracted confinement and boredom herself in the weeks leading up to the birth of Elizabeth Tudor, alongside the impending dread that childbirth normally entailed.

After her death Jane Seymour was given the full honours due to a deceased queen of England and was buried in St George's Chapel in Windsor Castle. Ten years later she was then accorded perhaps the highest honour of all of his spouses when Henry VIII was buried alongside her in 1547. They remain together there to this day, under the choir (or quire) in the aforementioned chapel, in what to all intents and purposes is a temporary vault. The grand tomb that the Tudor king envisioned for himself never came to pass, which may be a rather damning indictment of the view his children had of him, given that it was within their power to erect such a monument after he had passed away. Most visitors to Windsor Castle pass over the king's final resting place without even noticing the simple black slab that marks the spot:

IN A VAULT
BENEATH THIS MARBLE SLAB
ARE DEPOSITED THE REMAINS
OF
JANE SEYMOUR QUEEN OF KING HENRY VIII 1537
KING HENRY VIII
1547
KING CHARLES I
1648
AND

AN INFANT CHILD OF QUEEN ANNE.
THIS MEMORIAL WAS PLACED HERE
BY COMMAND OF
KING WILLIAM IV. 1837.

The king's grave – as well as that of Jane Seymour – lay undiscovered after the interment of the body of Charles I, until the entire vault was opened in 1813 in the process of renovations for a new, larger and more ornate royal vault. When they were replaced in 1888 a watercolour drawing of the contents was made by A.Y. Nutt, Surveyor of the Fabric to the College of St George. The picture shows a rather dank, confined little space, as well as revealing that Jane Seymour's coffin at least has remained relatively intact against the rigors of time. Henry VIII's coffin, on the other hand, has split asunder and appears to be covered with either rubble or fragments of wood. Whatever the detail, the overall impression is hardly an edifying one for someone with such a high opinion of himself. It's possible that the trestle supporting the king's coffin may have collapsed, although the picture doesn't seem to show a trestle actually supporting any of the coffins. On the other hand, it may have been accidentally damaged during the internment of the body of Charles I, or during that of the infant child of Queen Anne.

One can't mention this curiously damaged coffin without referring to a prophecy directed at the king while he was alive, courtesy of the Franciscan friar William Petow. Preaching at Greenwich during the Easter of 1532, Petow railed against Henry's efforts in setting aside Catherine of Aragon, as well as lambasting Anne Boleyn for putting forth 'the new religion'. He preached on a particular verse from the Bible – 1 Kings 22 – regarding King Ahab, who perished from the wounds that he suffered in battle. The verse reads: 'So the King died and was brought to Samaria, and they buried him there. They washed the chariot at a pool in Samaria (where the prostitutes bathed), and the dogs licked up his blood, as the word of the Lord had declared.'

Basically, Petow was comparing Henry to Ahab and Anne Boleyn to Ahab's wife, Jezebel, who was considered a false prophet because of her encouragement of the worship of Baal and Asherah, who were considered to be pagans and not the prophets of God who were traditionally worshipped by the people. Over time the name 'Jezebel' has come increasingly to be associated with either a fallen or a promiscuous woman, which ties rather neatly into the posthumous reputation of Anne Boleyn. However, Petow received rather a lenient punishment – a short prison term – for his incendiary sermon, before making good his escape to the Continent. When Henry VIII died the cortege carrying his body stopped for the night at Syon Abbey, where it was said that the coffin burst open, whereupon the oozing blood and matter was licked up by a dog that happened to be passing by, thus fulfilling Petow's prophecy. There may be some fact in this tale, given that dead bodies do sometimes swell up and then 'explode' due to a build-up of internal gases. Possibly the contents of the coffin simply began to leak and were indeed 'enjoyed' by some passing mutt. As ever, we shall likely never know for sure.

Chapter 16

Hacking the Head of Margaret Pole: Botched Executions

If you were to be beheaded by the orders of Henry VIII, then quite surely you wanted it done the way that it had been performed for Anne Boleyn; swiftly and mercifully despatched by sword. You did not want to endure your last moments on this mortal coil in the way that poor Margaret Pole did, being at the mercy of a blundering headsman who hacked at her neck and shoulders as though he were blind.

Margaret Pole, the Countess of Salisbury, was executed for treason on Tower Green in May 1541. She was sixty-seven years old at the time of her death, and as well as being one of the highest ranking and most respected noblewomen in all the country she was also one of the remaining members of the Plantagenet family, whom many considered to be the rightful rulers of England, and not the usurping Tudors. Margaret could claim a grand pedigree of descent as the daughter of the-then Duke of Clarence, who was brother to both Kings Edward IV and Richard III. Legend has it that the Duke of Clarence was drowned in a butt of malmsey in the Tower of London, on the orders of his brother, King Edward.

Following the end of the Wars of the Roses, Margaret Pole and her kin were forced to ingratiate themselves securely into the new Tudor regime, to such an extent that the countess was even given the role of governess to Henry's first daughter, Mary Tudor. Her actual tenureship in the role was somewhat chequered, due in part to Catherine of Aragon's dwindling marital fortunes and also because of the paths Margaret's own children, particularly her sons, chose in their respective lives – paths of conscience which would eventually bring them directly into collision with the iron will of the king.

Margaret's son Reginald Pole was dean in both Exeter and Dorset and had studied abroad for many years. The majority of his tuition fees were in fact paid by Henry VIII himself, before things turned sour between the two parties. However, like Thomas More, Bishop Fisher, the Carthusian monks and indeed countless others before him, Reginald Pole was opposed to the king's marriage to Anne Boleyn and also to the whole issue of the royal supremacy, and when asked to declare his support he instead chose to go abroad once more, this time into a kind of self-imposed exile. While abroad he went so far as to pen several tracts on the matter of the divorce from Catherine of Aragon which were then sent to the king back in England. To say that they were not well received is something of an understatement. Margaret Pole thus wrote several letters to her son, reprimanding him on his foolishness in risking the ire of the irascible Tudor king. Reginald Pole was still abroad at the time that his letters were received and digested, while his mother and the rest of the family were left in England to face the inevitable flack that followed their delivery. Reginald made a brief return to England but any attempt at a reconciliation with the king came to nothing. Not long after, he was made a cardinal by the Vatican, but then in 1539 disaster struck when his brother Geoffrey was arrested for corresponding with him.

It was around this time that Henry VIII tried to have Reginald Pole assassinated by covert means, but the attempts came to nothing. The countess and her other son Henry, Lord Montagu, were arrested soon after these frustrated attempts at assassination, although Geoffrey Pole was released after his testimonial implicated them in the correspondence with Reginald. Lord Montagu was executed and the rest of the family lost all of its lands and titles. Evidence was produced against Margaret Pole, including the discovery of a banner in one of her houses depicting the wounds of Christ, similar to the ones the rebels had marched under during the Pilgrimage of Grace several years previously. Reginald Pole had in fact been directed by the Pope to provide assistance to that particular rebellion, and so the link between mother and son as traitors to the Crown seemed clear and implicit.

The countess was left to languish in some considerable discomfort in the Tower of London for a total of two years before she herself was finally executed, on 27 May 1541. It was said that she pleaded her innocence to the last. Indeed, it was also said that when initially questioned that she 'fiercely denied any imputations against her. "We have dealt with such an one," her interrogator said, "as men have not dealt with tofore;

we may rather called her a strong and constant man than a woman"" (Ackroyd, 2012, p135).

When the countess was taken onto Tower Green to be executed she was forced to prostrate herself on the small block that had been set up for her. Again, the exact location of her execution is unknown but hers is one of the names that now adorns the glass memorial placed just in front of the church of St Peter ad Vincula. The headsman who was attending her was, by many accounts, an inexperienced youth who proceeded to hack at her neck and shoulders before she was finally dead – some say as many as ten strokes were needed to finish her off – while another tale has it that the countess leapt up after the first botched blow and was then pursued around the grass by the bungling young headsman wildly swinging his axe in her wake. Needless to say, the botched execution of an elderly and harmless woman who had offered years of loyal service to the crown went down rather sourly with Tudor social commentators, and merely cemented the view that the once fair and gallant Henry Tudor was turning fast into a paranoid and ruthless tyrant.

Margaret Pole was beatified as a Catholic martyr in 1886.

Chapter 17

The Licentious Life of Catherine Howard: Teenage Tudor Sexuality

Before she became Henry VIII's fifth wife, thus securing her place as the ageing king's midlife crisis, Catherine Howard lived a less than virginal life under the 'vigilance' of her father's stepmother, the Dowager Duchess of Norfolk. The dowager duchess had houses in Horsham and also at Lambeth, venues that were in essence supposed to serve as finishing schools for the sometimes surplus – i.e., often illegitimate – children of the nobility, and the young Catherine Howard probably alternated between the two locations as a child. Her father was Lord Edmund Howard and her mother was Joyce Culpepper.

It was quite common for the children from noble households to be sent to be supervised by the dowager duchess, to aid both in their upbringing and also their education, but her supervision was somewhat lax, and the children – both boys and girls – were pretty much left to their own devices. However, the houses in Horsham and Lambeth were not quite the dumping grounds for unwanted aristocratic bastards that some have made them out to be. As Catherine grew up, she noticed that it was common for some of the other girls in the 'dorms' to invite men into their company and also their beds after dark, and the young and impressionable girl soon fell into this mode of behaviour herself (at this stage she was barely in her early teens). Thus it came to pass that by the time she became Henry's wife, at the estimated age of just seventeen, she was already rather sexually well experienced, and far from being the 'rose without a thorn' that the poor, bloated monarch imagined her to be.

While living with the Dowager Duchess of Norfolk, Catherine first had a relationship with a music teacher called Henry Mannox, and then with one of the duchess's secretaries, Francis Dereham. The relationship with Dereham went much further than the juvenile fumblings she had enjoyed with Mannox and Catherine may even have allowed herself to have become precontracted to him. They certainly referred to each other on occasion as 'husband' and 'wife' and formed some sort of a plan to live together on a more permanent basis once they were a little older. The relationship was almost certainly sexual, if testimony later given by Catherine's 'friends' is to be believed. Their affair lasted for several years and only came to an end when Catherine won the coveted position as a lady-in-waiting to Henry VIII's fourth wife, Anne of Cleves.

It was while working in this position that she caught the king's eye, in much the same fashion as her cousin Anne Boleyn had first supplanted Catherine of Aragon. Catherine Howard soon saw off her mistress and became the next queen of England – they were married at Oatlands Palace in Surrey – but there were apparently few ill feelings between the two women. They even danced together at Christmas, a first for a pairing of Henry's ill-starred spouses.

Henry himself was apparently delighted with his new bride, simpering over her and pawing her in public whenever he felt the fancy. However, it wasn't long before Catherine began a clandestine relationship with Thomas Culpepper, one of the king's young favourites. Culpepper was a gentleman of the king's privy chamber, and despite the fact that he may have been involved in the rape of a park keeper's wife and the murder of a villager – accounts differ as to whether it was him or a brother with the same name – a pardon was given and he duly rose in royal favour.

At the same time that Culpepper was in the ascendancy, Catherine was being blackmailed by members of the dowager duchess's old household, who were seeking positions in her new and far more prestigious abodes. One of these was none other than Francis Dereham, and appointing him as her secretary was, alongside the Culpepper affair, one of the stupidest mistakes of Catherine's young, naïve life. The 'lewd and licentious' life of Catherine Howard – who happened to come from a staunchly Catholic family – then came to the attention of the piously Protestant Archbishop Cranmer, who promptly reported his concerns to the king in a letter he left on a nearby seat in the royal chapel at Hampton Court Palace. Cranmer maintained that the matters concerning the life of Henry's 'rose without a thorn' were so grievous that he had not the heart to impart them to the king face-to-face. The guilty parties were promptly rounded up, and it was at this point that Catherine's relationship with Culpepper came out into the open, shortly after her doings with Dereham were made known to the king. Legend has it – i.e., take it with yet another hearty pinch of salt – that on her arrest Catherine broke free from her guards and dashed screaming down what is now known as the Haunted Gallery at Hampton Court, desperate to reach the king while he was at prayer in the royal chapel. Ghost stories have abounded about the location ever since, with people purporting to 'feeling faint' and the like. What seems more certain is that the king was so moved by her betrayal that he wept openly before his council, lamenting his lack of good fortune in the marital department.

After his arrest, Francis Dereham confessed that he had once had a relationship with the queen before she actually became the queen, but maintained – truthfully, one imagines – that his current employment as her secretary was on a purely platonic basis. Given the butchery of the Boleyn faction in 1536, to hint at anything further would have been tantamount to suicide. Archbishop Cranmer looked for evidence of a precontract between Catherine and Dereham but could find none. It is possible that this evidence may have been destroyed by the dowager duchess when she got wind of what was happening at court. Catherine and the other culprits in the sexual conspiracy – more slut-shaming – were all questioned, and a letter to Thomas Culpepper from Catherine was found which pretty much sealed her fate on that score. It remains a rather touching little missive, currently preserved in the National Archives at Kew:

Master Culpepper,

I heartily recommend me unto you, praying you to send me word how that you do. It was showed me you were sick, the which thing troubled me very much till such time that I hear from you praying you to send me word how that you do, for I never longed so much for a thing as I do to see you and to speak with you, the which I trust shall be shortly now. That which doth comfortly me very much when I think of it, and when I think again that you shall depart from me again it makes my heart to die to think what fortune I have that I cannot be always in your company. It my trust is always in you that you will be as you have promised me, and in that hope I trust upon still, praying that you will come when my Lady Rochford is here for then I shall be best at leisure to be at your commandment, thanking you for that you have promised me to be so good unto that poor fellow my man which is one of the griefs that I do feel to depart from him for then I do know no one that I dare trust to send to you, and therefore I pray you take him to be with you that I may sometime hear from you one thing. I pray you to give me a horse for my man for I had much ado to get one and therefore I pray send me one by him and in so doing I am as I said afor, and thus I take my leave of you, trusting to see you shortly again and I would you was with me now that you might see what pain I take in writing to you.

> Yours as long as life endures.
> Katheryn.

One thing I had forgotten and that is to instruct my man to tarry here with me still for he says whatsomever you bid him he will do it.

Thomas Culpepper was executed for his affair with the queen but was shown the mercy of the axe rather than suffering the full horrors of a traitor's death, as befell poor Sir Francis Dereham, who had supposedly 'spoiled' Catherine for the king in the first place. After being initially imprisoned in Syon Abbey, Catherine Howard herself was then taken to the Tower of London, and finally executed on Tower Green on 13 February 1542. In the days leading up to her execution she had requested that the executioner's block might be placed in her room, the better that she might be able to position herself upon it, in order to present a noble spectacle when finally she was beheaded. Meanwhile, Henry VIII showed what was fast becoming his trademark callousness where a condemned wife was concerned: 'On the same day (as Catherine's death warrant became law), the King held a banquet to show his lack of concern. In his own mind at least, he was still young and virile, and needed to be seen as such, therefore inviting 50 ladies of the court to dine with him with "great and hearty cheer"' (Denny, 2008, p245).

Chapter 18

The Madness of Lady Rochford: A Tudor Take on Mental Illness

The woman referred to by some writers – particularly Julia Fox – as 'the notorious Lady Rochford' was in fact Jane Boleyn, formerly Parker, Anne Boleyn's sister-in-law, wife to Anne's beloved brother George. She was the daughter of Baron Morley, born in Norfolk sometime around 1505. Through her mother she was actually a very distant relative of Henry VIII, but this was not uncommon at the time. She served in some capacity or other to his first wife, Catherine of Aragon, before continuing in the same fashion for her successor, Anne Boleyn. She married Anne's brother George several years before Anne herself became queen.

Jane initially secured her place in the Tudor temple of infamy when she was one among several who gave evidence of a perceived incestuous relationship between her husband and his sister during the probable Cromwell-orchestrated coup against the Boleyn faction in 1536. Her words were roughly to the effect of 'his tongue in her mouth and her tongue in his mouth', and so on and so forth, in the sort of lurid detail that the Tudors secretly adored behind their pious and often blank expressions; quite probably Cromwell himself provided the more lurid details.

Jane's marriage to George Boleyn was not a 'love-match' by any stretch of the imagination and there is no evidence that it produced any children either. George Boleyn had a reputation as rather an ardent womaniser, and a posthumous but unverified reputation as a lover of men also, not to mention the fact that he was supposedly an ardent beau of his sister to boot. However, there is no evidence that he raped his wife either – as shown in the second season of *The Tudors* – and also no real evidence that he was having it away with the musician Mark Smeaton on the side. George Boleyn was in his prime when the Buggery Act of 1533 was passed, so putting it around amongst variously inclined men at the court may not have been the wisest of career moves. Having said that, the Buggery Act basically prohibited the activity between a man and a woman also, as well as with an animal:

An acte for the punyshement of the vice of buggerye. Cap. vi.

For as moche as there is not yet sufficient & condigne punishment appointed & limitted by the due course of the lawes of this realme for the detestable & abominable vice of buggeri committed with mankind or beest. It may therefore plese the Kings Highnes, with the assent of his lordes spiritual & temporal & the Commons of this present parliament assembled, that it may be enacted by authorite of the same, that the same offence be from hensforth adjuged felony, and suche order and fourme of proces therin to be used ageinste the offendours, as in cases of felonie at the common lawe. And that the offenders being herof convict by verdicte, confession, or outlaurie, shall suffer suche peynes of dethe, and losses, and penalties of their goodes, cattals, dettes, londes, tenements, and heredytamentes, as felons benne accustomed to do accordynge to the order of the common lawes of this realme. And that no person offendynge in any suche offence, shalbe admitted to his clergye, And that justices of peace shall haue power and auttoritie within the limittes of theyr commissions and jurisdiction, to here and determyne the sayde offence, as they use to do in cases of other felonies. This acte to endure tyll the laste daye of the next parlyament.

Jane Boleyn survived the subsequent scandal that brought down most of the Boleyn family, and then went on to serve as lady-in-waiting to Henry's three subsequent wives: Jane Seymour, Anne of Cleves, and Catherine Howard respectively. But it is with Henry's fifth wife, the aforementioned teen queen Catherine Howard, that her licentious reputation as 'the notorious Lady Rochford' really cemented itself into the popular historical psyche. Quite why Jane Boleyn did what she did has remained a source of curiosity – and often downright astonishment – to historians ever since. The explanations are abundant, but none of them really ring true.

Catherine Howard, perhaps somewhat perturbed by her ageing husband's obesity, ulcerated leg, and terrific Tudor temper, was tempted by one of the dashing young men of the king's chamber, Thomas Culpepper. Catherine and Culpepper carried on a clandestine relationship that could only have flourished with Lady Rochford's connivance (see in particular the love letter from Catherine to Culpepper in the previous chapter) as Lady Rochford waited on the queen and basically controlled all entry and exit from her presence. When the entire court went on a great progress to the north in the summer of 1541, Lady Rochford was charged by the queen at the various stopping points with finding appropriate places for the courting couple to rendezvous, a variety of romantic boltholes which included on occasion a back staircase and also a toilet (still extant). On one occasion, when Henry VIII came a-calling to claim his own conjugal rights, Lady Rochford even had to bar the door to the room in which the couple were canoodling with her own body. If *The Tudors* TV series is to be believed then Lady Rochford took a vicarious, peeping-tom style pleasure in bringing the queen and Culpepper together, and quite frankly this explanation is a little bit better than those concocted by some 'eminent' historians who have dismissed her antics as little more than those that might erupt on occasion from any high-class bawd.

The fact that Lady Rochford went mad in the Tower of London after her arrest suggests a far more fractured personality, although whether this fact was discovered when she was found to be smearing her own faeces over the walls of her cell, again as *The Tudors* suggests, is perhaps open to a little more artistic interpretation. Quite possibly, Catherine Howard brought her influence to bear on the older woman and simply *ordered* her to arrange the various liaisons with Culpepper, but this is all conjecture. In the final analysis, no one really knows what compelled Lady Rochford to act as she did, be it salaciousness, audacity, mental illness, or perhaps even some curious combination of all three. Or perhaps it was quite something else altogether, some snippet of historical reference as-yet undiscovered by historians, some feud or happening that forged her personality in a particular fashion. Certainly, Catherine Howard was a mere novice in the ways of court intrigues, whereas Lady Rochford was a seasoned practitioner in the art. Anyone who could survive 1536 and then go on to retain a position so close to the Crown for several years thereafter had to be doing *something* right.

The Madness of Lady Rochford: A Tudor Take on Mental Illness

Lady Rochford was executed, along with her mistress on Tower Green on 13 February 1542. There was a law in place before her arrest that prohibited the execution of an insane person roughly along the lines of 'diminished responsibility', but Henry VIII was so incensed at the role that Lady Rochford had played in his latest cuckolding scandal that he had it repealed just so that she might be beheaded. Despite her 'newfound' insanity, Lady Rochford apparently made a fairly coherent scaffold speech, and today her name is commemorated alongside that of Catherine Howard, Anne Boleyn and Margaret Pole, among others, on the elegant glass memorial erected on Tower Green. The best attempt to rehabilitate her character to date has come from the aforementioned biographer Julia Fox, who trawled all of the extensive propaganda that has percolated around Lady Rochford's memory for the last few hundred years, and then wrote a spirited defence of her sometimes mindless machinations; 'Whatever she had done wrong, and it was in fact very little, she paid the price. Her life was stolen from her. So was her story' (Fox, 2008, p326).

Chapter 19

Henry VIII's Horrible Leg

Henry VIII is almost as famous for his gammy, ulcerated leg as he is for the fact that he had six wives and spent a great deal of time wrenching England away from Rome simply so that he could get his first divorce.

Apparently, he first injured his leg in a jousting accident some time during the 1520s, but the more serious fall in January of 1536 – the shock of which *may* have caused Anne Boleyn to miscarry – opened up the old wound and from then on it became ulcerated on a regular basis and never really healed. From time to time the wound became clogged up with fluids and the resultant ulcers failed to burst, causing the king excruciating pain. Further pain would follow when the newly formed ulcer would then have to be lanced and all of the pus drawn out (several of the later episodes of *The Tudors* TV series convey such scenes in painstakingly graphic detail). On one occasion, the infection spread so much that the king was said to have turned completely black from head to toe – other sources say it was simply in the face – and it was thought, not unsurprisingly, that he had not long left to live. He may, in this instance, have contracted blood poisoning or septicaemia. In which case the treatment that might save his life would involve, as said, the ulcer first being lanced and then drained of all the offending yellow pus, after which a poultice – herbs or such-like wrapped in a warm compressed cloth – would be administered and then held in place over the wound by means of a bandage. Sometimes the ulcers were lanced with red-hot pokers, which also served the purpose of cauterising the wound before possible infection could set in. Again, there was no pain relief to speak of while this procedure was being performed.

Up until relatively recently it was thought that the role of Catherine Parr, Henry's last wife, was to administer poultices to his gammy leg on a regular basis, and little else besides. It is only relatively recently that historians have begun to distance themselves from her reputation as 'the nursemaid' wife and allow her to come into her own as an accomplished woman of considerable education; the first queen of England to publish a book, no less. In fact, it was often the role of Henry's male attendants –

including the disgraced Thomas Culpepper of Catherine Howard fame – to tend to the dressing of the wound and also to administer whatever pain relief means were available.

It has famously been suggested that Henry rejected his fourth wife Anne of Cleves, because he considered her to be too ugly – 'a Flanders mare' – and also because she had 'strange and unusual odours about her', as well as sagging breasts and a flabby stomach, but it may be that it was *she* who was in fact repulsed by the morbidly obese monarch with his suppurating, ulcerated leg. Therefore, it came to pass, possibly, that on their divorce it became merely a matter of royal spin to turn her into a monster so that the king didn't lose face. Quite how much face Henry had left to lose in the wake his alleged repeated cuckolding courtesy of Anne Boleyn is another matter entirely. In this way, *her* disgust was therefore turned into a fictional dislike on Henry's part, which the king could wield as a propaganda weapon to hide the fact that she had perhaps been horrified by him. Either that, or perhaps she really did look nothing like her rather comely miniature by Holbein. History, as they say, is written by the winners, and most often by the blokes.

Towards the end of his life, the combination of the king's weight – he never stinted on the vast amounts of food and drink paraded before him – and his weakening legs meant that by the end of his life Henry was practically immobile. The fact that he went to France in 1544 to wage war is nothing short of a miracle, and one must feel immensely for the poor horses that had to ferry his bloated bulk around on the inhospitable, war-torn terrain. However, on returning to England mobility soon became even more of an issue and he had to be almost winched in and out of bed, with said winch also apparently being used to get him on and off his horse. A specially constructed chair was also used to carry him around, and it was even said that 'the ground shook when he moved' (Baldwin Smith, 2010, p119). Given the lack of painkillers available in Tudor times – there were natural remedies aplenty, but certainly no ibuprofen – it is somewhat understandable that the pain sometimes drove him to distraction, and he became increasingly irascible and even on occasion downright sociopathic. One can hardly imagine the Henry Tudor of some thirty years previous vindictively passing a new law on the execution of the insane simply in order to satisfy his bloodlust where a former lady-in-waiting to his various wives was concerned. He died from natural causes on the 28 January 1547.

Chapter 20

When Catherine Parr Lost Her Head: Toxic Politics at the Tudor Court

'Divorced, beheaded, died; divorced, beheaded, survived.' So goes the old rhyme about the fates of Henry VIII's six wives, but aside from the startling symmetry between the fates of wives one to three and then four to six, it may not be so well known that Catherine Parr – the sole 'survived' – nearly didn't survive at all, and in fact came very close to being the third wife that Henry VIII would have sent to the executioner's block.

His sixth and final queen was a very learned woman, and a devout Protestant to boot. She was also the author of several books, a singular feat for an English queen at the time: *Prayers or Meditations* was published posthumously, but her second book, *The Lamentations of a Sinner*, was published in 1548, not long after Henry VIII had died. Therefore, given her learned background, it was small wonder, during her tenure as Henry's sixth wife, that Catherine Parr felt that she was on fairly steady ground when she decided that it was time to lecture the king on ridding England of the 'dregs of popery'. Unfortunately, however, Catherine had powerful Catholic enemies in the court, among them Bishop Gardiner, a man who had been percolating around the royal court for a great deal longer than she herself had.

As far as the Catholic faction – and Bishop Gardiner – were concerned, Catherine had also been indiscreet, at the very least, in her sympathy for Anne Askew, the Protestant preacher who was the only woman ever to be racked in the Tower of London. Anne askew was a lifelong Protestant, divorced from her Catholic husband and spreading the word regarding what she considered the falsity of the Catholic doctrine of transubstantiation, among others. She was originally from Lincoln, but events soon drew her to London, where she took to preaching what she perceived to be the true religion with increased vigour. Such outspokenness brought her to the attention of both the authorities and also of the more sympathetic factions at court, Catherine Parr amongst them. Anne Askew was arrested several times and was eventually taken to the Tower of London, where she became – aside from Margaret Cheyne – the only woman ever to be tortured. Margaret Cheyne had been involved to some extent with the Pilgrimage of Grace, and after being imprisoned in the Tower of London she was eventually burnt for heresy.

Anne Askew was questioned while at the Tower by privy councillor Richard Rich, a man whose former credits also involved the betrayal of Thomas More, despite the fact that Rich basically remained a Roman Catholic himself for his entire life. Regarding the interrogation of Anne Askew, Rich was assisted by Lord Chancellor Wriothesley, both of them basically playing 'bad cop' as they tried to coerce Anne into naming the women supporting her from within the confines of the court (money had been sent to support Anne during the length of her confinement in the Tower, emanating from gentlewomen connected with Catherine Parr's privy chamber). After an initial bout of questioning, Anne Askew was taken to one of the lower rooms in the White Tower and shown the rack, as an incentive to make her confess. When she refused to implicate anyone, she was asked to undress – except for her shift – and was then fastened to the rack and questioned once again. She recalled what happened next in her own words:

> then they put me on the rack because I confessed no ladies
> or gentlewomen to be of my opinion; and there they kept me
> a long time, and because I lay still and did not cry, my lord
> chancellor and Master Rich took pains to rack me with their
> own hands till I was nigh dead. Then the lieutenant (of the
> Tower) caused me to be loosed from the rack. Immediately,
> I swooned away, and then they recovered me again. After
> that I sat two long hours reasoning with my lord chancellor
> upon the bare floor.

Her words neglect the unsavoury details; that the lieutenant of the Tower baulked at such a task, and that Rich and Wriothesley thus rolled up their sleeves and operated the mechanism of the rack themselves. Anne Askew's body was lifted slowly above the bed of the rack and then held quite taut. A further turning of the wheel proceeded to stretch her to the point where her joints began to pop, one by one by one. The aforementioned lieutenant of the Tower, Sir Anthony Knyvett, was so distressed by what he witnessed that he took his concerns directly to Henry VIII himself. The king was apparently also rather concerned by the methods of torture being used upon a woman, although the fact remains that Knyvett had allowed Rich and Wriothesley to proceed with the application of the rack in the first place. As Linda Porter has pointed out, 'he (Knyvett) must have had a high-level mandate; chillingly, it is certainly possible that the king himself had authorised the violence meted out to Anne' (Porter, 2010, p264–5). As mentioned in the chapter on Mark Smeaton, Anne Askew's injuries were so grievous that she had to be carried to the pyre on which she was to be burnt in a chair. The burning itself took place at Smithfield on 16 July 1546 (on the site of the current Smithfield Meat Market). She was condemned to the flames along with three other Protestants and, as stated, gunpowder was quite possibly secreted about their persons in order to finish them off more mercifully. Whether the gift of the gunpowder came courtesy of one of the gentlewomen of Catherine Parr's privy chamber we shall never know.

The situation for Henry VIII's final wife was escalating rapidly, proceeding so far on the part of her enemies that an arrest warrant was actually drawn up for the queen as suspicions about her Protestant leanings grew. However, on its way to being delivered, the warrant for the queen's arrest was dropped and then found by one of Catherine's ladies (there lingers a slight whiff of incredulity about these proceedings). After recovering from the initial shock of finding out that she was to be arrested and put on trial, Catherine concocted a story to tell the king when he undoubtedly came to confront her with evidence of her misdemeanours. When the actual moment came, Catherine played up to Henry's monumental male ego with admirable artfulness, telling him that she had only engaged in 'contentious' religious discourse with him in order to take his mind off the suffering caused by his ulcerated leg, and that as a woman she, of course, had no real knowledge of any such things whatsoever. Quite succinctly put, this finessed example of feminist survival in such a male-dominated arena had 'the whispering ghosts of Catherine of Aragon, Anne Boleyn and Jane Seymour (all three of whom had learnt in their various ways of the king's impatience with female argument) would certainly have counselled this tactful allusion to that theological expertise on which the King prided himself' (Fraser, 1993, p475–6). Luckily for Catherine, Henry was in a mood to believe her, and the guards who later came to try and arrest her as she was walking with the king were quickly chased away. The fact that they weren't called off beforehand remains further testimony – if any were needed – to how sullen and vindictive Henry VIII had become in his dotage.

Chapter 21

Admiring the Admiral: Elizabeth Tudor and Thomas Seymour's Immoral Liaison

After her father Henry VIII's death, the young Elizabeth Tudor – in her early teens at the time – was sent to live with the last of her many stepmothers, the widowed former queen of England, Catherine Parr, and her new husband, Thomas Seymour. Seymour was brother to Henry VIII's third wife, Jane, and also 1st Baron Seymour of Sudeley. To add to his titles he was also Lord High Admiral of England. Added to this, he was also said to be handsome, dashing and rather charismatic, although by all accounts there was little of real substance up top. However, to an impressionable young girl like Elizabeth Tudor, who had been so recently bereaved of her all-powerful father, he would have seemed like an ideal repository for all of those confusing feelings of adolescent anxiety.

The problem sprung from the fact that Seymour, despite being married to Catherine Parr, most definitely had an eye on Elizabeth in return, most likely as a stepping stone to further success. As a result, the new living arrangement was all but doomed from the outset. Elizabeth was, at this stage in her life, the third in line to the throne of England, but being several years younger than her stubbornly Catholic half-sister, Mary, she was also – at least for Seymour – a more enticing prospect for ascending the greasy Tudor pole to real power. By modern standards Elizabeth was still basically a child, but the Tudor age of consent was considerably more flexible than the current modern-day equivalent. Certainly, it appeared that Seymour himself wasn't going to let a little thing like a rather dubious age gap get in the way of his ambition.

It was said that Thomas Seymour would walk into Elizabeth's bedroom early in the morning, wearing only his night shift – an unflattering gown that stretched from the neck right down to the toes – and that he would proceed to slap her about the buttocks and then 'come at her' in her bed.

Elizabeth soon countered this behaviour by making sure that she was up bright and early and already busily at her studies when he arrived. Such prudence shows that, whatever girlish feelings she may have harboured for him secretly, she was not prepared to forsake her reputation for the sake of a quick fumble. Quite likely, Elizabeth may also have been simply fearful of his approaches, worried that what seemed as horse-play on the surface may soon have escalated into something far more serious.

On one memorable occasion, immortalised countless times in the various TV and film adaptations of her life, he also decided to take a pair of scissors to the dress Elizabeth was wearing and literally cut her out of it, helped on this occasion by none other than his wife, Catherine Parr, who held the struggling girl while he played the 'practical joke'.

Catherine Parr was probably just taking part in the sort of high-spirited horse-play that was not an uncommon form of humour for the times, but it wasn't long before she found her step-daughter and her husband in a slightly more amorous clinch and was thus forced to send Elizabeth away from the house as a result, not merely to save her marriage but also to salvage the young girl's reputation. Catherine Parr had been previously warned of what was going on by Elizabeth's governess, Kat Ashley, but had dismissed the woman's tales, suspecting that Kat secretly had a crush on Thomas Seymour herself (there may have been some truth in this).

In Tudor times, girls were considered marriageable by the age of twelve, whilst for boys the age considered suitable was fourteen. Nevertheless, most marriages contracted at such a young age were often not consummated until the individuals were a little older, hence the problems regarding Catherine of Aragon's virginity in regard to her marriage to Arthur Tudor. Poor Margaret Beaufort, the mother of Henry VII, gave birth before she was even thirteen years of age.

Guidelines on sexual intercourse were laid down strictly by the church. The missionary position was the only one considered 'moral', and any children who were conceived outside of this stricture were said to be doomed to deformation. However, for women in Tudor times there was at least the boon that it was considered necessary for both participants to reach a climax in order for them to conceive successfully. Birth control was illegal as such, because sex outside of marriage was deemed unlawful and sinful. However, birth control measures were fairly common amongst the various classes, including the method of the man withdrawing from the woman before ejaculation, while the woman might line her vagina with swabs doused with herbs, peppers, or wool soaked in vinegar; such things were said to stop the sperm cold in its tracks. Rather riskier, the woman might also insert beeswax into her vaginal canal in order to clog up the entrance to the cervix.

It wasn't long after Elizabeth left Catherine Parr's household, taking up residence within the house of Sir Anthony Denny, that Catherine herself gave birth to a baby girl. She then died several days later from 'childbed fever', almost certainly the same infection that had finished off Jane Seymour over a decade earlier. Despite Catherine Parr's 'survived' status as the sixth and final wife of Henry VIII, there is still an uncanny symmetry to the way that fate handled the various outcomes of the six wives of the tyrannical Tudor king, numbers three and six both dying shortly after childbirth, while numbers two and five were beheaded, and numbers one and four were both 'disposed of' via divorce.

It was said of poor Catherine Parr on her deathbed that she became feverish and delusional, speaking many bitter words to her husband about how he had mistreated her during the course of their marriage. These were probably veiled references to the fact that he clearly had harboured a 'thing' – be it passionate or just plain political – for the fiery flame-haired girl who had been expelled from their house so recently. Catherine's daughter, called Mary, is believed not to have lived long past the age of two.

Now a widower, Thomas Seymour soon set his sights more firmly on the young Elizabeth Tudor. He was helped in this regard by Kat Ashley, whose opinion of him seemed suddenly to have performed an abrupt about-turn: 'despite her earlier qualms, she was obviously attracted to Seymour herself, and something of his creepy sexiness comes out in his message to her, "whether her great Buttocks were grown any less or no?" Quite what Seymour did to these two intelligent women who were supposed to have Elizabeth's welfare at heart is impossible to know, but Katherine Ashley now proved herself as much of an idiot as the dowager queen had been' (Hilton, 2014, p70). Seymour also began to work himself up toward the goal of snatching the reins of power from his brother Edward, who had risen to the position of Lord Protector of England since the death of Henry VIII. He began ingratiating himself with their nephew, the young Edward VI, mainly by giving him cash presents. Apparently one of the boy's main complaints was that his uncle

Edward was rather parsimonious when it came to forking out pocket money from the royal purse.

Things came to a head in January 1549 when Thomas Seymour organised a minor coup by actually trying to abduct the young king from his apartments in Hampton Court Palace, and in the melee and panic he shot and killed the boy's pet dog. Following this, Seymour was arrested and taken to the Tower of London to await trial. Among those questioned about their relationship with the now-disgraced admiral was the young Elizabeth Tudor. She found herself for the first time facing the sort of adversity that would eventually come to shape her into the shrewd political operator and consummate monarch that she eventually became. Kat Ashley was also arrested, along with several other members of Elizabeth's household, but despite a relentless barrage of questioning – including the allegations of flirtations with Seymour – the young Elizabeth handled herself with considerable aplomb, fending off the various attacks and slurs against her honour, and in the end the whole lot of them walked free.

Thomas Seymour was executed on 20 March 1549.

Chapter 22

The Lamentable Lady Jane Grey

Lady Jane Grey, the famous 'nine days queen', could be considered England's first queen regnant; that is, if one doesn't take into account the 'reign' of Matilda some 300-odd years earlier. However, most serious historians place the woman who came after Jane Grey, 'Bloody' Mary Tudor, as being the first true queen regnant of England, thus categorising Jane's brief reign as something of a historical curiosity. Jane was forced onto the throne of England at the tender age of just sixteen or so – her exact birth date is an issue of some dispute – and less than a year later she was dead, executed on Tower Green by the new Catholic regime, blindfolded and apparently groping for the executioner's block, a picture of pure tragic poetry that would inspire portrait painters for centuries to come.

To begin with, Jane was the daughter of Frances Brandon, the eldest daughter of Henry VIII's sister Mary, by her husband, Charles Brandon, the Duke of Suffolk, who was memorably portrayed by 'Superman' hunk Henry Cavill in *The Tudors*. Jane's royal pedigree was therefore almost impeccable, especially as Henry VIII's will – disputed as it often was – had effectively ruled out the succession of the offspring of his other sister, Margaret, and their descendants. Margaret Tudor had married James IV of Scotland back in 1503 and was therefore the grandmother of Mary Queen of Scots, who would go on to devoting most of her adult life to trying to win the English crown that she believed was rightfully hers. When Edward Seymour, the Lord Protector of England, was executed, the power base around the young king Edward VI shifted over to the Duke of Northumberland, and he began to make his own plans for perverting the line of succession in such a way that would see him gain control of the crown in England. Northumberland had been among those who had helped to oust Edward Seymour from power, promptly becoming the new protector for the young king. Edward Seymour actually survived his initial fall from grace but an attempt to win back his old office and bring down Northumberland's new regime saw him sent to the scaffold in 1552.

In May 1553 Jane was married to Guildford Dudley, one of the sons of the Duke of Northumberland. By now Northumberland was indeed effectively ruling England for the teen King Edward VI, who was showing the first serious signs of the illness that would soon finish him off, thus paving the way for Northumberland's schemes to reach fruition. Young Guildford Dudley was one of the brothers of the future Elizabeth I's favourite, Robert Dudley. The fact that the Duke of Northumberland was Robert's father meant that the traitor's pedigree of Robert's family would plague him to varying degrees throughout his life, and probably had a small part to play in the fact that he never became Elizabeth Tudor's official consort.

The marriage between Guildford and Jane Grey brought the young Jane effectively under Northumberland's direct control, and from there he was then able to exercise his influence over the by-now mortally ill Edward VI, convincing him to change the order of succession, eliminating both his half-sisters, Mary and Elizabeth, from succeeding to the throne. In the words of the historian Alison Weir, Northumberland was 'anxious to remain in power and determined that the Lady Mary, an ardent Catholic, should never have the opportunity of overthrowing the Protestant religion established under Edward VI' (Weir, 2008, p15).

There has been some dispute with what Edward VI actually died from at such a tragically young age, but the roughly common consensus seems to be that he was laid low either by tuberculosis or perhaps an unspecified disease of the lungs. He had measles and smallpox a year or so before his final illness, a combination which most certainly would have left him open to more serious afflictions in taking hold. Measles often suppresses the immune system for quite some time, even after the illness in question has since passed. Several years earlier Edward had been laid so low by some mysterious, secret illness that his doctors had not expected him to survive. In fact, it seems that poor Edward had never enjoyed good health. He was so short-sighted that doctors were taken to treating his poor eyes with some sort of balm or unguent, and besides this he was also said to be somewhat deaf.

Whatever the cause of his final illness, it began with a fever and a cough during January of 1553, and from that point his condition worsened quickly. His half-sister Mary came to visit him at around this time, and he spent the entirety of the meeting bedridden and suffering from a cough so violent that it made conversation at times almost impossible. He was also said to have difficulty in breathing, although at times he was well enough to walk outside, and to attend to matters of state from the safety of his sickbed. There were rumours circulating that he had been poisoned, but such comments were pretty much the norm in a time when a great many illnesses were inexplicable and unable to be cured by the rather primitive medicines then in use.

By June, after rallying several times, his condition had worsened still further and he was vomiting fluids of various colours, from green and brown all the way down to a pinkish bloody substance. Medical expertise, such as it was, now considered him to be suffering from an affliction, possibly a tumour, on the lung, and it was at this point that his doctors declared that there was little to no hope of his making any sort of a recovery. Not long after this, poor Edward's legs swelled to such a size that he was permanently confined to his bed. This swelling was said to have been caused by allowing a stranger – a woman – to administer her cures upon him, which had rather an adverse effect rather than that undoubtedly intended. If this story is indeed true, it shows quite how desperate people were to preserve the life of this poor, beleaguered boy.

By now, Edward himself seemed also to have lost the will to live. Tragically, he was said to have whispered to his tutor, John Cheke, 'I am glad to die.' His stomach also swelled up and various sores began to break out all over his body, although these may have been bedsores and not a direct symptom of the illness itself. He now found sleep almost impossible, and could only be given rest by the administration of various opiates, and any food he might take he soon vomited back up again. His fever was almost constant, and sometimes it became violent in intensity. He was no longer able to use the toilet, but when he did manage to pass fluids or a motion, they were said to be possessed of the most terrible stench. Also, his hair began to thin and then fall out altogether, as did his nails. When he made his final appearance, at a window of Greenwich Palace on 1 July, the onlookers were said to be appalled by his 'thin and wasted' condition. Painkillers and palliative medicines were primitive at best, and he suffered greatly in the days leading up to his death, even losing the ability to speak. He died in the arms of Sir Henry Sidney, a childhood companion, at Greenwich Palace, five days after his deathly appearance at the window.

When Edward eventually died, as per the stipulations of his freshly altered will, Jane Grey was hastily proclaimed queen of England and taken to the Tower of London to begin her reign in relative seclusion and safety. However, popular support for Mary Tudor as the 'legitimate' next in line was already growing. As a result, Jane's 'reign' ended up lasting for a mere nine days, all of which she spent shut up in the Tower of London while the battle for the crown raged outside. When it became clear that Mary Tudor had both might and right on her side, the Privy Council effectively abandoned Jane Grey and switched their allegiance to Mary instead. The proclamation in London on 19 July 1553 that declared her as the next rightful queen of England was greeted with jubilation. Jane and her husband went from being the country's premier royal couple to being its top royal prisoners. They were kept stewing in the Tower of London while the Duke of Northumberland was executed for the part that he had played in trying to pervert the proper order of royal succession (there were apparently 10,000 witnesses to his demise, on 22 August 1553).

In November 1553 the hapless young royal wannabes themselves were tried at the Guildhall and found guilty of high treason. Following that, they were promptly sent back to the Tower of London, but the conditions of their confinement were not unduly harsh. However, the advent of the Wyatt Rebellion, the popular widespread protest against Mary Tudor's plan to marry Phillip of Spain, saw both Jane and Guildford executed as a kind of panicked 'precautionary measure' against the possibility that the rebels would win and then perhaps set them up as king and queen. More likely, the rebels' actual plan was to put the young Elizabeth Tudor on the throne, which in turn led to her own precautionary imprisonment in the Tower at the time.

Guildford Dudley was executed first, taken from the main edifice and up onto Tower Hill on 12 February 1554, aged only eighteen or nineteen. Shortly before his execution he had asked to see his wife one last time, but Jane had refused, unable to bear the bittersweet sorrow of such a meeting. The cart carrying his remains back into the Tower of London passed directly below the windows of the rooms where his wife was confined. She observed the grim procession from the window and is said to have proclaimed tearfully, 'Oh Guildford, Guildford!!'

Lady Jane Grey herself was executed within the relative privacy of Tower Green on the very same day, and only a short while after having caught sight of her husband's decapitated body. She gave a short scaffold speech to those assembled which went roughly along the lines of: 'Good people, I am come hither to die, and by a law I am condemned to the same. The fact, indeed, against the Queen's highness was unlawful, and the consenting thereunto by me: but touching the procurement and desire thereof by me or on my behalf, I do wash my hands thereof in innocency, before God, and the face of you, good Christian people, this day.' She then pleaded with the executioner to do away with her quickly and placed her blindfold provided for such occasions over her eyes herself. However, she was then unable to find the block on which she was to be beheaded and ended up groping around on her hands and knees on the scaffold in search of it, a pitiful sight that was, as said, to go on to inspire portrait painters for centuries to come. The lieutenant of the Tower helped her into the proper position, after she had begun crying out, 'What shall I do? Where is it?!' Shortly afterwards all such considerations were well beyond her. Both she and her unfortunate husband – as well as her ambitious father-in-law – were buried in the chapel of St Peter ad Vincula, alongside so many other unfortunate casualties of the Tudor reign.

The sisters of Lady Jane Grey, Catherine and Mary, also suffered dark and ultimately tragic fates as a result of their proximity to the crown. Catherine married Edward Seymour, son of the Lord Protector Edward Seymour, without the consent or even the knowledge of the-then queen Elizabeth I. Notoriously insecure about her right to the throne, Elizabeth was, in the eyes of Catholicism, a bastard and a usurper. After all, she promptly had the couple tossed into the Tower of London and then ordered that they should be closely monitored. While she was a prisoner, Catherine nevertheless managed to conceive not one but *two* sons by her husband, but she was never released, setting a something of a grim precedent where Elizabeth and her shaky royal succession was concerned. Mary Queen of Scots would suffer a similar fate when she sought refuge in England a few years later, although her tenure around the Midlands would prove to be far more protracted.

Poor Catherine died at the age of just twenty-seven, almost certainly of consumption. She is buried in Salisbury Cathedral, along with her husband. Consumption was the Tudor name for what is known medically today as tuberculosis. 'TB' affects the lungs, with major symptoms including a vicious cough which often brings up blood. Another symptom was severe weight loss, which led to the illness being given the name 'consumption', in that it was perceived that the body appeared to be devouring itself from within.

Mary Grey also had a claim to the throne, but unlike her sisters was apparently far less of an appealing prospect, with her diminutive stature, 'displeasing' features, and an apparent hunchback. However, this didn't stop Mary from bagging the 6ft 8in tall Thomas Keyes, Elizabeth I's serjeant porter, in 1565. The fact that there had been no witnesses to her sister Catherine's wedding had enabled the crown to have it annulled and the offspring declared illegitimate, so Mary wisely took the precaution of making sure that there were appropriate witnesses to her nuptials. Nevertheless, this didn't stop the wrath of Elizabeth from descending on her and summarily dissolving the union. Keyes was committed to the Fleet Prison while poor Mary was promptly placed under strict house arrest. The Fleet Prison stood beside the River Fleet – the largest of London's subterranean rivers – in the Farringdon/Clerkenwell area and was demolished in 1846. It was known for being a particularly arduous place of confinement, with inmates often subjected to any number of cruelties by their jailers.

Mary Grey and Thomas Keyes were never to lay eyes on each other again. Poor Mary was shuttled around the houses of various of the nobility, almost always as an unwelcome guest, 'with all her books and rubbish'. However, by considerable determination she eventually managed to inveigle herself back into the queen's household and even gained a position as one of her maids-of-honour; this was around 1573. She died, quite possibly of the plague, in 1578, and was buried in Westminster Abbey in the tomb of her far more illustrious mother.

Chapter 23

Burn, Baby, Burn! The Monstrous Reign of 'Bloody' Mary Tudor

Mary Tudor, daughter of Henry VIII and his first wife, Catherine of Aragon, came to the throne in 1553 on a wave of popularity following the swift suppression of the schemes of the Duke of Northumberland. All of this followed the death of her younger half-brother, Edward, and the aforementioned brief 'reign' of royal 'wannabe' Lady Jane Grey.

Discounting Jane – not to mention Matilda – Mary Tudor was therefore England's first real queen regnant. A patriarchal society the Tudors may have been, but the right to rule by birth right was essentially undisputed, whether the monarch in question was a man or a woman. However, the problem stemmed from the fact that Mary was also a staunch – some might even say a fanatical – Catholic, and at that point England was a newly Protestant country. This was due to the fact of her father's break with Rome and his divorce from her mother, a process continued by her half-brother's strict adherence to the new faith. Poor Edward VI had even gone to the lengths of nominating an 'outside favourite' – i.e., Jane Grey – simply in order to stop his pious Catholic half-sister from succeeding to the throne.

Although, on her accession, Mary initially professed tolerance for all Protestants, it wasn't long before major Protestant figures such as Hugh Latimer and Archbishop Thomas Cranmer found themselves imprisoned. They would go on to suffer the same fate as almost 300 other heretics whom Mary ordered be burned alive for refusing to recant of their beliefs, or 'heresy'. However, in terms of the Tudor timeline she was not a pioneer in this method of purging an unclean house of its dregs. Thomas More had famously employed the same tactics when dealing with the first wave of Protestants to wash up on England's shores some thirty years previously, and fire was considered by far the best way of sending these poor, misguided souls to meet their maker. So feared were Mary's methods that even Elizabeth Tudor, that covert champion of the Protestant cause who many saw as waiting in the wings, was forced to make a show of compliance with the new regime, although Elizabeth was able on one occasion to fake a stomach-ache shortly before she was to attend mass. Although they had been relatively close when Elizabeth was younger, the advent of adulthood – alongside the inevitable differences in faith – saw herself and Mary drifting apart to a degree that eventually became decidedly dangerous for Elizabeth. Thereafter, Mary viewed both her sister's Protestantism and her covert popularity with the people of England with an intense, almost paranoid, suspicion.

The first executions of Protestants occurred in 1555, and soon no less a personage than Archbishop Thomas Cranmer himself was forced to watch as Bishops Latimer and Ridley were burnt at the stake ahead of him. Cranmer recanted his 'heresy' and reluctantly rejoined the Catholic faith, but perhaps because of his pivotal role in securing her father's divorce from her mother Mary refused to pardon him. He too then went to the stake, whereon he promptly withdrew his recantation. Cranmer had in fact recanted of the Protestant faith several times before his death, but as he was actually surrounded by the flames he recanted his recantations and stuck his right hand into the heart of the fire, quite possibly seeking to punish the hand that had written down said recants in the first place.

Together, Cranmer, Ridley and Latimer became known as the 'Oxford Martyrs', because of where they were burned. The exact spot is on Broad Street in Oxford, not far from the main shopping thoroughfare, and is today marked by a small plaque which is known as the 'Martyr's Cross'. There is, however, a far larger monument to the three men, complete with statues, nearby on the intersection of Magdalen, Beaumont and St Giles Streets. Given that Cranmer was one of those instrumental in securing Henry VIII's divorce from Mary's mother, Catherine of Aragon, alongside securing the king's new marriage to the usurping Anne Boleyn – and allowing for a little imaginative license – it's not entirely impossible to imagine Mary beaming with delight as news of his demise was delivered to her.

Estimates of the exact number of people who were burnt at the stake during Mary's reign vary slightly between 283 and around 300. Possibly the most horrific of all the burnings that were carried out was that of Perotine Massey from Guernsey in the Channel Islands. Perotine, her sister, Guillemine, and their mother, Catherine, were all convicted of heresy and sentenced to be executed by fire on 18 July 1556. Perotine was heavily pregnant when she went to the stake. Although the women were all meant to have been strangled as they were tied to the stake, the rope securing them broke and they all apparently tumbled headlong into the flames. Perotine gave birth while being burned alive. The new-born baby – said to have been a boy – was initially rescued from the fire before orders were given that the child should be cast into the pyre as well. It may be worth adding that the reporting of this particular atrocity was attacked by the Catholic priest Thomas Hardly, who disagreed with the recording of the event by the Protestant propagandist and historian John Foxe. Harding stated that had Perotine proclaimed her pregnancy then the executions would most certainly have been postponed until after she had given birth. Basically, Harding was saying that the death of her baby was down to Perotine herself, although this is hard to square with the fact that she would have been visibly with child at the time of the burnings and mercy ought to have been shown on that account alone. These women are now known as 'The Guernsey Martyrs', and there is a monument to them at Saint Peter Port, the capital of Guernsey, near to the site of the execution. It was said that 'the stubborn determination of the Queen, so merciful in every other matter, showed not only the strength of her feelings but the courage they had suffered in the treatment of her mother and herself. The force of her nature had hitherto shown itself in courage and patience; now it was seen in another aspect' (Jenkins, 1965, p54).

It takes little imagination to consider what these poor unfortunates – indeed, what all of the victims of Mary's religious intolerance – must have gone through. One need only wave a finger above the naked flame of a candle to understand the smallest portion of the pain they must have endured. There was, as previously mentioned, always the hope that the executioner would be merciful – with monetary encouragement – to secure the prisoner in such a way that they would be strangled before they suffered too much. Sometimes – and it is sincerely to be hoped – the prisoners might also have suffocated from the sheer amount of smoke caused by the burning of the pyre to which they were affixed. A burning on a wet day was to be particularly dreaded, because the dampness meant that the pyre would blaze far more slowly, thus prolonging the suffering even further. A burning on a windy day, however, could oftentimes be considered a mercy, as it might cause the conflagration to consume the unfortunate victims far quicker; fanning the flames, basically. There was also the previously mentioned fact that gunpowder might be administered to the pyre or else secreted on the bodies of one or all of the victims in order to hasten their departure.

The mass burnings of Protestants, far from bringing England flocking back into the Catholic fold, merely hardened the hearts of the general public against Mary, and she went down in history with the nickname of 'Bloody Mary'. However, the drink that shares the unfortunate sobriquet is not in fact named after her, despite some of the more imaginative labels adorning the bottles on display on various supermarket shelves. The ruthless failure of Mary's reign effectively signed the death warrant for any further Catholic rule in England, something that Mary Queen of Scots was to find out to her cost several years later when she found her somewhat impeccable candidacy to the succession all but overlooked by an overly hostile Protestant Privy Council. There have been various attempts to rehabilitate Mary's reign and achievements over the years, and to concentrate on that fact of her being England's first queen regnant, but the stain of vicious, merciless Protestant slaughter stills hangs heavy upon her, much as the beheading of several of his wives lingers over her famous father.

Chapter 24

The Curious Case of the Phantom Foetus: 'Bloody' Mary Tudor's Gynaecological Traumas

Aside from ordering the burning of cartloads of bothersome Protestants, Mary Tudor's other main occupation during her brief reign was getting herself pregnant and thus providing England with the secure male heir that it needed to carry her beloved Catholic faith into the future. The trouble began when it became obvious that Mary's husband, Phillip II of Spain, was slightly less enamoured of his middle-aged, dumpy, and rather dourly devout bride than she was with him. Despite this, Mary soon believed that she had fallen pregnant and the whole of England held its collective breath and awaited news of a royal heir in the cradle. Her body was rapidly showing all of the signs of pregnancy, including the fact that she had ceased 'to bleed', as the Tudors politely termed the cessation of a woman's natural cycle. Also, she experienced what she became convinced were several bouts of morning sickness and a conviction that she could feel the child growing inside her.

This was in September 1554. By April 1555 there was still no sign of a child, but the court – not to mention Mary herself – believed that the birth was imminent. All due preparations were made and she took to her chambers to await the delivery. By the end of June there was still no sign of a child and so hopes began to fade. The queen and her swollen stomach – abdominal distension, most likely – held out for another month or so before it became apparent that there would definitely be no baby. Almost on cue, Mary's stomach began to slowly deflate, alongside her rapidly dwindling hopes. In fact, a swollen stomach is one of the most common symptoms of a phantom pregnancy, although the bump is caused not by a baby but instead by a build-up of gases, or sometimes by fat or by faeces. However, so convincing are the perambulations of the phantom infant that various women have sincerely reported feeling it kick or move inside them. This may indeed have been the case where Mary was concerned. The majority of false pregnancies have no physical cause but are, for the most part, brought on by a period of psychological instability, often where the intense desire to conceive a child is the underlying culprit of said instability.

Phillip II left the country soon after Mary failed to give birth, ostensibly to fight a war against the French, and Mary was left heartbroken and then depressed in his wake. The patriarchal pressure on her to produce an heir was duly redoubled, with Mary interpreting her failure to conceive as being due to God's wrath in not adequately ridding her realm of heretics.

After Phillip paid a brief visit to his wife in 1557 she soon began to believe that she was pregnant for a second time, even though the tallying of the dates with regards to conception were slightly askew. However, no one was about to point this out to Mary when she was clearly pinning all her hopes on this being the real deal, even if to the rest of the court it might have seemed more like some sort of a comical immaculate conception. As the 'pregnancy' progressed, it started to become clear that instead of expecting a child Mary was in fact fatally ill, and by the autumn of 1558 it was even clearer that she did not have long left to live.

At this point her court began deserting her in droves, in order to go and pay homage to her successor, her younger half-sister, Elizabeth. Also, at this point 'Phillip sent his confessor Fresneda to England to urge Mary to send a message to Elizabeth recognising her as heir to the throne. Mary refused, and broke out in a rage. She told Fresneda that Elizabeth was not her sister or the child of Henry VIII, but the daughter of an infamous woman who had outraged the Queen her mother and herself. Fresneda persisted, and at last Mary agreed to do as he asked; but two days later she changed her mind, and again refused' (Ridley, 2002, p72).

In the end, Mary Tudor died a tragic and lonely death in St James' Palace on 17 November 1558. Yet again, the exact cause of her death is somewhat unclear, but it may have been from uterine cancer. She had pleaded with her half-sister beforehand to leave the newly reminted Catholic religion as it was, and in her usual prevaricating way Elizabeth Tudor had answered her by not really giving any concrete answer at all. Mary had stipulated in her will that she wished to be reunited in death with her mother in Peterborough Cathedral, but in the end she was interred in Westminster Abbey, eventually to share a tomb with the half-sister of whom she had been at first so fond, and then later so very suspicious.

Chapter 25

The Wyatt Rebellion

The Wyatt Rebellion broke out in 1554, led partly by Thomas Wyatt the younger, son of the famous poet Thomas Wyatt, the man who had once been so very besotted with Anne Boleyn. The burnings of Protestants which were to characterise Mary Tudor's reign hadn't yet commenced when the rebellion began. Instead, the Wyatt Rebellion was in fact a form of protest against the fact that Mary was going to marry Phillip II of Spain, who was both a foreigner and, of course, a devout Catholic. Parliament, and the country, would much have preferred Mary to marry an English prince, one such as Edward Courtenay, who possessed countless royal connections. Mary, however, preferred her Spanish prince, because of his Catholicism and also because she was herself half-Spanish through her mother, Catherine of Aragon.

Mary's bloody-mindedness where the issue of her potential husband was concerned was simply the first of her countless personal and political misfires. To say that she lacked the personal touch of her half-sister, Elizabeth, is something of an understatement. The idea of a rebellion to overthrow Mary's reign was hatched by Thomas Wyatt the younger, and also Sir James Croft, Sir Peter Carew, and Henry Grey, 1st Duke of Suffolk, among others. Implicit in their plan was the idea to replace the hopefully deposed Mary with her younger Protestant half-sister. Elizabeth's complicity in the Wyatt Rebellion is doubtful, but not impossible, although that uncertainty didn't save her from having to endure an excruciating stint in the Tower of London at the height of the alarm. As a result of the rebellion both the deposed Jane Grey and her husband were also executed. Though they had both been charged with treason there had been some hope that their lives would be spared, at least until the rebellion broke out and they were seen by Mary's regime as potentially dangerous replacements for the queen.

Elizabeth Tudor was brought to London and then committed to the Tower because of her alleged complicity in the plot. She famously sat

Above left: Richard III. (Public Domain, from the British Library's digital collection, 015115658)

Above right: Cardinal Wolsey statue, Ipswich. (Author's own)

Dismemberment by horses. (Jacques Onfroy de Bréville, Public domain, via Wikimedia Commons)

Left: Thomas More.
(Public Domain, from the
British Library's digital
collection, 015264398

Below: Execution plaque,
Tower Hill. (Author's own)

Sir William Stanley, K.G.	1495
James Tuchet, 7th Baron Audley	1497
Edward Plantagenet, Earl of Warwick	1499
Edward Stafford, 3rd Duke of Buckingham	1521
John Fisher, Bishop of Rochester	1535
Sir Thomas More	1535
Thomas Darcy, Lord Darcy of Templehurst, K.G.	1537

Execution of Carthusian Monks. (Mary Evans Picture Library)

THE RACK.

The Rack. (Public Domain, from the British Library's digital collection, 014939336)

ANNA·BULLEYN, *Gemalinne van* HENDRIK.DE VIII.
Koning van Engeland. binnen Londen onthalst.

Above left: Scavenger's Daughter. (Nighthiker, CC0, via Wikimedia Commons)

Above right: Anne Boleyn's Execution. (Jan Luyken, Public domain, via Wikimedia Commons)

Coffins of Henry VIII and Jane Seymour. (Public domain, via Wikimedia Commons)

Above: Margaret Pole's botched execution. (Public domain, via Wikimedia Commons)

Right: Ulcerated leg. (Wellcome Collection: St Bartholomew's Hospital Archives & Museum CC BY 4.0)

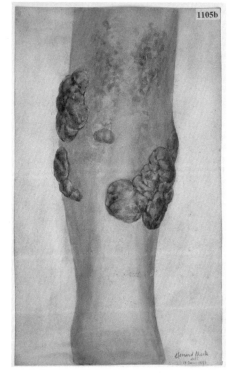

Anne Askew on the rack. (Public domain, via Wikimedia Commons)

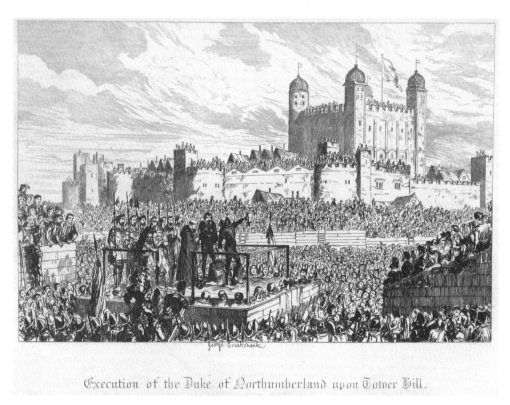

Execution of the Duke of Northumberland upon Tower Hill.

Tower Hill execution of the Duke of Northumberland. (Public Domain, from the British Library's digital collection, 014803715)

Above: The poetical portrait of Lady Jane Grey's execution. (Paul Delaroche, Public domain, via Wikimedia Commons)

Right: Thomas Cranmer meets his end. (Joseph Martin Kronheim (1810-1896), Public domain, via Wikimedia Commons)

Inhuman execution of a mother, two daughters, and an infant at Guernsey, in 1556. page 419.

Above: The Guernsey Martyrs.
(John Foxe, Public domain, via
Wikimedia Commons)

Left: Amy Robsart's mysterious death.
(William Frederick Yeames, Public
domain, via Wikimedia Commons)

Decurforium in quo Rex Henricus ii. mortifero vulnere fauciatur, die vlt. Iunii. 1559.

Above: The jousting match in which Henri II of France was injured, Paris 1559. (Wellcome Collection CC BY 4.0)

Right: Catherine de Medici. (Public Domain, from the British Library's digital collection, 014885431)

NOSTRADAMUS

Above left: Nostradamus. (Public domain, via Wikimedia Commons)

Above right: Francis II. (Author's own)

BEAR-BAITING, AS PRACTISED IN THE TIME OF QUEEN ELIZABETH.

Bear Baiting - circa 16th century. (Mary Evans Picture Library)

LORD DARNLEY.

Right: Lord Darnley. (Public Domain, from the British Library's digital collection, 014871374)

Below: Mary Queen of Scots witnessing the murder of David Rizzio. (John Opie, CC0, via Wikimedia Commons)

THE MURDER OF DAVID RIZZIO.
On the 9th of March 1566.

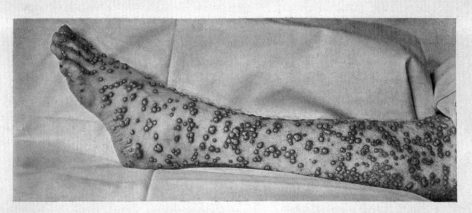

Early pustules of smallpox. (Wellcome Collection CC BY 4.0)

The aftermath of Kirk o' Field, as sent to William Cecil. (Wellcome Collection CC BY 4.0)

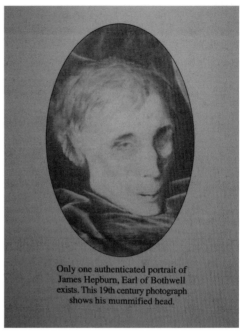

Only one authenticated portrait of James Hepburn, Earl of Bothwell exists. This 19th century photograph shows his mummified head.

Above left: Carberry Hill monument. (Author's own)

Above right: Portrait of the Earl of Bothwell taken 300 years after his death. (From the collections of Scottish Borders Council. Copyright administered on behalf of Scottish Borders Council by Live Borders)

Mary Queen of Scots escapes from Loch Leven. (Edward Leahy, Public domain, via Wikimedia Commons)

Little Ease dungeon, Tower of London. (J Valentine & Co, Public domain, via Wikimedia Commons)

Mary Queen of Scots' execution. (Public Domain, from the British Library's digital collection, 014939995)

Fotheringay Castle remains. (Author's own)

English fire ships fend off the Spanish Armada. (Public domain, via Wikimedia Commons)

The death of Elizabeth I. (Paul Delaroche, Public domain, via Wikimedia Commons)

down on the rain-soaked steps at Traitor's Gate and refused to proceed any further, until coaxed into her lodgings by the Constable of the Tower. The day before she was taken to the Tower, Elizabeth had managed to delay her imprisonment by penning what has come to be known as the 'Tide Letter'. Elizabeth knew that passage along the Thames depended very much on the ebb and flow of the tide, and therefore that if she could delay her journey there by writing a letter pleading for mercy then there was a chance that her half-sister might listen to her petition and then grant her an audience:

> If any ever did try this old saying, "that a king's word was more than another man's oath," I most humbly beseech your majesty to verify it to me, and to remember your last promise and my last demand, that I be not condemned without answer and due proof, which it seems that I now am; for without cause proved, I am by your Council from you commanded to go to the Tower, a place more wanted for a false traitor than a true subject, which though I know I desire it not, yet in the face of all this realm it appears proved.
>
> I pray to God I may die the shamefullest death that any ever died, if I may mean any such thing; and to this present hour I protest before God (Who shall judge my truth, whatsoever malice shall devise), that I never practised, counselled, nor consented to anything that might be prejudicial to your person any way, or dangerous to the state by any means. And therefore I humbly beseech your majesty to let me answer afore yourself, and not suffer me to trust to your councillors, yea, and that afore I go to the Tower, if it be possible; if not, before I be further condemned. Howbeit, I trust assuredly your highness will give me leave to do it afore I go, that thus shamefully I may not be cried out on, as I now shall be; yea, and that without cause.
>
> Let conscience move your highness to pardon this my boldness, which innocency procures me to do, together with hope of your natural kindness, which I trust will not see me cast away without desert, which what it is I would desire no more of God but that you truly knew. Which thing I think and

believe you shall never by report know, unless by yourself you hear. I have heard in my time of many cast away for want of coming to the presence of their prince; and in late days I heard my Lord of Somerset say that if his brother had been suffered to speak with him he had never suffered; but persuasions were made to him so great that he was brought in belief that he could not live safely if the Admiral lived, and that made him give consent to his death. Though these persons are not to be compared to your majesty, yet I pray God the like evil persuasions persuade not one sister against the other, and all for that they have heard false report, and the truth not known.

Therefore, once again, kneeling with humbleness of heart, because I am not suffered to blow the knees of my body, I humbly crave to speak with your highness, which I would not be so bold as to desire if I knew not myself most clear, as I know myself most true. And as for the traitor Wyatt, he might peradventure write me a letter, but on my faith I never received any from him. And as for the copy of the letter sent to the French king, I pray God confound me eternally if ever I sent him word, message, token, or letter, by any means, and to this truth I will stand in till my death. Your highness's most faithful subject, that hath been from the beginning, and will be to my end, Elizabeth I humbly crave but only one word of answer from yourself.

The letter had no effect on what little remained of Mary's mercy, and once in the Tower, Elizabeth was examined in much the same diligent manner that she had faced in the wake of her alleged 'affair' with Thomas Seymour. Her interrogators found that the wily girl had grown into an accomplished young woman: 'There was even a moment when she had the mastery – when the dark-bearded Earl of Arundel suddenly dropped to his knees, and exclaimed: "Your grace saith true and certainly we are very sorry to have so troubled you with so vain matters!"' (Ross, 2005, p48). Nevertheless, her stint in the Tower of London served merely to temper the steely personality of the young woman who was to succeed to the throne of England far sooner than anyone at that time dared imagine.

The rebellion had already taken hold in Wyatt's native Kent and the rebels soon began a march on the capital, but in London Mary Tudor rallied her forces with a sterling speech given at the Guildhall, and from then on the tide seemed suddenly to turn in her favour. The rebels reached the outlying areas around the centre but found themselves unable to enter the city and occupy it. Unable to take the capital by force, the rebellion rapidly began to dissipate. Thomas Wyatt the younger surrendered and was shortly executed, but not before he was brutally tortured in the hope of implicating the imprisoned Elizabeth, something that he either could not or would not do. Had he in fact succumbed then the history of England would have been quite different. Many of the other rebels were executed with him, many of the men hung, drawn and quartered and their remains pinned up at various points throughout the city as a grim reminder to those left behind of what exactly were the consequences of rebellion against the renewed Catholic regime.

Elizabeth herself remained in the Tower of London for a short duration, during which time she was again questioned repeatedly about the extent of her involvement in the Wyatt Rebellion. Again she managed to evade the clumsy probings of her interrogators. Eventually, she was released from the Tower and put under house arrest at Woodstock. She spent nearly a year there, her health see-sawing with the stress of it all, until eventually her brother-in-law, Phillip, persuaded his wife to set her free.

Chapter 26

What Really Happened to Amy Robsart

After Elizabeth I ascended to the throne in 1558 it wasn't long before it became clear that Robert Dudley, son of the traitor Duke of Northumberland, was her favourite. Dudley was tall, dashing, and had an extremely well-turned calf (the male Tudor calves were the equivalent of the much sought-after six-pack for any self-respecting modern-day metrosexual man). But Dudley also came complete with a wife, one Amy Robsart, the couple having in fact been married since 1550. It was, from all accounts, a love-match rather than the typical Tudor matrimonial affair conducted mainly for business or social connections. Amy Robsart was born in Norfolk in 1532, making her just a year older than Elizabeth, so Amy wasn't quite eighteen when she married Dudley.

Elizabeth soon made Robert Dudley her Master of the Horse, a post which – probably quite intentionally – required almost constant attendance upon the queen, and as a result he saw very little of his wife, who was left to languish in various residences north of London, culminating in her final, fateful stay at Cumnor Place, near Abingdon. It was here that her dead body was discovered at the bottom of a flight of stairs on the 8 September 1560. She had been left alone in the house shortly before her body was discovered, while her maids all went out to enjoy the fun of a nearby fair. It had been reported in court circles that she had been ill for some time – 'a malady in one of her breasts' was the more accepted story – and it had been said rather scandalously that the queen would marry Robert Dudley as soon as Amy was decently dead and buried. In the wake of her actual death these remarks of course took on a much more sinister meaning, given that she hadn't passed away in a peaceful manner (i.e., propped up in bed by pillows and surrounded by friends and family). Instead, it appeared that she had been the victim of some sort of foul play. The gossip about her mysterious death soon gathered pace, and it wasn't long before even Mary Queen of Scots was remarking that Elizabeth and her horse master had jointly done away with his wife so that they could be married, therefore legalising their illicit liaison.

An inquest was held into Amy Robsart's death, and the verdict given was that the whole thing had been a tragic accident: no one – and that included Robert Dudley in particular – was in any way to blame for what had happened to her. However, the gossip simply would not go away, and Elizabeth was forced in the end to distance herself from Dudley in order to save her own reputation. (A lesson she tried years later to share with her cousin Mary Queen of Scots when she too found herself in a similar situation with the Earl of Bothwell, though with little success.) Sir William Cecil, Elizabeth's chief advisor and secretary of state, had no love for Dudley and had apparently told sources, including the Spanish ambassador, that Amy Robsart had not been ill at all. He claimed that a rumour had been 'put about' that she was unwell, perhaps with the intent that she might have succumbed to some sort of foul play on the part of persons 'unknown' with the story of her illness being used as a convenient cover.

However, it may have been that Amy Robsart really was ill, and that supposition has led some historians to conjecture that Amy had committed suicide because she knew herself to be dying, and also because she despaired at the fact that her husband had effectively dropped her in favour of the queen. Some historians have also speculated that Sir William Cecil himself might have arranged for her assassination, knowing the irreparable damage it would do to the reputation of Robert Dudley and his ambitions to become king, a series of events that would forever put the kibosh on any sort of formal relationship between himself and Elizabeth. Indeed, the trauma of what happened to his wife would haunt Dudley for the rest of his days. The Spanish ambassador De Quadra 'thought it was murder and so did the scandal-mongers. This view of the matter found expression fifty years later on the London stage: "The surest way to chain a woman's tongue is break her neck, a politician did it"' (Read, 1965, p201).

The detection and treatment of cancer in all its myriad forms was its infancy during Tudor times, but doctors and surgeons were aware of the disease. Indeed, it was thought then that breast cancer, from which Amy may well indeed have been suffering, was caused by a clotting of milk in the mammary gland. It has been speculated that Henry VIII's elder brother, Arthur, may in fact have died from testicular cancer, and also that Catherine of Aragon – as previously mentioned – may have perished from cancer of the heart. There were no treatments for the disease in Tudor times, and with sanitation so poor there were no options for any sort of surgery either. However, there seems scant evidence that the Tudors lived in such dread of the disease as do their twenty-first century descendants. For the most part, that particular dread was reserved for the likes of the Sweating Sickness, smallpox and consumption/tuberculosis.

Chapter 27

Splinters and Sorcerers

While England see-sawed between Catholicism, Protestantism, and then back and forth again, as the differing power struggles were played out between the various children of Henry VIII, Mary Queen of Scots spent an idyllic childhood mostly situated in the lush and verdant Loire Valley in France, engaged to Francois, the future king of France. She'd been sent to France as a small child to keep her out of her great uncle Henry VIII's clutches, back when he wanted her betrothed to his son Edward. In France, Mary was the darling of the French court, spoilt and pampered, and apparently indulged in all her wishes. It was the life of a fairy-tale princess, only for real, and this period in her life was turned into a teen drama called *Reign* for The CW network in the US. The famous 'Four Maries', her childhood companions Mary Beaton, Mary Seton, Mary Fleming and Mary Livingston, were 'reimagined' in the show for a modern audience as 'Greer', 'Kenna', 'Lola', and 'Aylee', although quite which is which might leave even the most ardent of historians baffled. The best way to approach *Reign* is to try to forget everything you know about Mary and take it simply as the vaguely surreal offspring of *Sex and the City* and *Game of Thrones*.

Mary's husband-to-be, the future Francis II, was far from a fairy-tale prime-time TV prince, however. He was small, underdeveloped, and often unwell with various ailments. In stark contrast, Mary herself would reach almost 6ft as a grown woman and even as a child she towered over her fiancée, taking on a role more akin to that of a big sister than that of an actual prospective spouse. They were eventually married in a lavish ceremony on 24 April 1558 at Notre Dame Cathedral. Soon afterward, Mary would find herself catapulted from the already exalted position of French princess par excellence to that of being the actual queen of France itself, but that was still to come. It didn't bode well for the occasion of the wedding that Mary had chosen to wear white, the traditional tone for brides in the present day but back then considered the official French colour of mourning.

However, white was the colour that set Mary's marvellous complexion off to its best effect. Her skin was said to be almost translucent, so much so that you could see the veins in her throat, and so it was white that she wore on her first wedding day. The respective roles of the newly married royal couple as the future queen and king of France seemed on that day a long way distant, and they looked forward to a fruitful future spent idling their days away back in the Loire valley, a veritable cosseted courtly couple. Fate, however, had other ideas in mind.

On 30 June 1559 Henry II of France, father to Mary's young husband, received a serious head injury during a jousting match which had been held as part of the celebrations for the treaty of Cateau-Cambresis, and also to celebrate the marriage of his daughter Elisabeth Valois with Phillip II of Spain, Mary Tudor's widowed husband. Elisabeth was one of Mary Queen of Scots' closest childhood friends during her time in France. Henry's wife, the calculating Catherine de Medici, had begged her husband not to ride in the jousts that day, having foreseen his demise with the aid of her astrologer entourage, among them the master necromancer Nostradamus.

*****

Nostradamus was born in 1503 in Provence, one of nine children. He studied at the University of Avignon but was forced to flee due to an outbreak of the plague. He then became an apothecary, during which time he invented a 'rose pill' that could supposedly ward off the plague. As he grew older, his interest in conventional medicine dwindled as his interest in the occult grew ever stronger, turning his talents towards horoscopes and eventually the predictions for which he would become famous. It was then that he published his most famous book, *The Prophecies*. It contained several hundred quatrains (stanzas), all of which purport to foreshadow various future events, some of them quite pertinent either to the present day or recent twentieth-century history. Among others, he was said to have forecast the rise of Adolf Hitler, as well as predicting the 9/11 terrorist attacks. However, the various prophecies are vaguely worded and open to any number of interpretations. Aside from predicting that the French king would perish during a joust, Nostradamus also apparently foresaw the Great Fire of London, as well as the French Revolution, which happened some several hundred years after the death of Henry II of France. The prophecy for this particular historical upheaval read as follows:

> From the enslaved populace, songs,
> Chants and demands
> While princes and lords are held captive in prisons.
> These will in the future by headless idiots
> Be received as divine prayers.

The 'enslaved populace' would be the Third Estate, who took control of Paris and then issued their demands to the royals, i.e., the princes and lords. The remark about 'headless idiots' is quite easily interpreted as someone falling victim to the guillotine. Regarding the rise of Adolf Hitler, Nostradamus is said to have written:

> From the depths of the West of Europe,
> A young child will be born of poor people,
> He who by his tongue will seduce a great troop;
> His fame will increase towards the realm of the East.

> Beasts ferocious with hunger will cross the rivers,
> The greater part of the battlefield will be against Hister.
> Into a cage of iron will the great one be drawn,
> When the child of Germany observes nothing.

Whilst the gist of the prophecy may appear on the surface to be true, there are some rather glaring inconsistencies with the life of the real Adolf Hitler, who was in fact born of middle-class parents and not the prophecy's purported 'poor people'. However, the line about 'by his tongue will seduce a great troop' seems to be a clear indication of Hitler's renowned oratory prowess in regard to stirring up the German nation to side with him against the perceived enemy. As for 'Hister', well, that is not a misspelling but rather the Latin word for the River Danube, which flows through ten countries, including Germany. Nostradamus is also said to have predicted the advent of the atomic bomb:

> Near the gates and within two cities
> There will be scourges the like of which was never seen,

Famine within plague, people put out by steel,
Crying to the great immortal God for relief.

The phrase 'within two cities' is the standout one here, given that it was two cities – Nagasaki and Hiroshima respectively – that were struck with the first atomic bombs at the end of the Second World War, in 1945. Those who didn't perish in the initial blast often died from radiation poisoning, which may therefore be read as the line, 'crying to the great immortal God for relief'. Japan also suffered a food shortage in the aftermath, which may be linked to the word 'famine', but there is no apparent explanation for the word 'plague', unless one also tacks the idea of radiation poisoning onto that, as well as the aforementioned line regarding 'the great immortal God'. Finally, there is the idea that Nostradamus also predicted the 9/11 terrorist attacks:

Earthshaking fire from the centre of the Earth
Will cause tremors around the New City.
Two great rocks will war for a long time,
Then Arethusa will redden a new river.

The reference to the 'New City' itself is fairly obvious, while the 'two great rocks' might be taken for the twin towers themselves, although they didn't really 'war for a long time' as such; that may refer more to the conflict between America and Islamist ideology that erupted in the wake of the atrocity. The line about 'fire from the centre of the earth' doesn't seem relevant unless one buys into one of the many conspiracy theories regarding 9/11, whereby this line may be construed as referring to the covert – and controlled – detonation of the twin towers by the American government.

The reception to the various works of Nostradamus in his lifetime was mixed, to say the least. Indeed, he was summoned to Paris by Catherine de Medici, whereupon she asked not only for an explanation for the various predictions, but also that he should then draw up a horoscope for each of her many children. Such was the esteem in which she held him that Catherine eventually appointed him physician-in-ordinary to her son Charles IX of France. All of the prophecies were laid out before Henry II in a preface to the 1558 edition of the book, intended as a tribute to the French king:

TO THE MOST INVINCIBLE
MOST POWERFUL AND MOST CHRISTIAN
HENRY, KING OF FRANCE THE SECOND:
MICHEL NOSTRADAMUS,
HIS VERY HUMBLE AND VERY OBEDIENT
SERVANT AND SUBJECT,
WISHES VICTORY AND HAPPINESS

Ever since my long-beclouded face first presented itself before the immeasurable deity of your Majesty, O Most Christian and Most Victorious King, I have remained perpetually dazzled by that sovereign sight. I have never ceased to honour and venerate properly that date when I presented myself before a Majesty so singular and so humane. I have searched for some occasion on which to manifest high heart and stout courage, and thereby obtain even greater recognition of Your Most Serene Majesty. But I saw how obviously impossible it was for me to declare myself.

While I was seized with this singular desire to be transported suddenly from my long-beclouded obscurity to the illuminating presence of the first monarch of the universe, I was also long in doubt as to whom I would dedicate these last three Centuries of my prophecies, making up the thousand. After having meditated for a long time on an act of such rash audacity, I have ventured to address Your Majesty. I have not been daunted like those mentioned by that most grave author Plutarch, in his Life of Lycurgus, who were so astounded at the expense of the offerings and gifts brought as sacrifices to the temples of the immortal gods of that age, that they did not dare to present anything at all. Seeing your royal splendor to be accompanied by such an incomparable humanity, I have paid my address to it and not as those Kings of Persia whom one could neither stand before nor approach.

It is to a most prudent and most wise Prince that I have dedicated my nocturnal and prophetic calculations, which are composed rather out of a natural instinct, accompanied by a poetic furor, than according to the strict rules of poetry. Most of them have been integrated with astronomical calculations corresponding to the years, months and weeks of the regions, countries and most of the towns and cities of all Europe, including Africa and part of Asia, where most of all these coming events are to transpire. They are composed in a natural manner.

Indeed, someone, who would do well to blow his nose, may reply that the rhythm is as easy as the sense is difficult. That, O Most Humane king, is because most of the prophetic quatrains are so ticklish that there is no making way through them, nor is there any interpreting of them.

Nevertheless, I wanted to leave a record in writing of the years, towns, cities and regions in which most of the events will come to pass, even those of the year 1585 and of the year 1606, reckoning from the present time, which is March 14, 1557, and going far beyond to the events which will take place at the beginning of the seventh millenary, when, so far as my profound astronomical calculations and other knowledge have been able to make out, the adversaries of Jesus Christ and his Church will begin to multiply greatly.

I have calculated and composed all during choice hours of well-disposed days, and as accurately as I could, all when Minerva was free and not unfavorable. I have made computations for events over almost as long a period to come as that which has already passed, and by these they will know in all regions what is to happen in the course of time, just as it is written, with nothing superfluous added, although some may say, There can be no truth entirely determined concerning the future.

It is quite true, Sire, that my natural instinct has been inherited from my forebears, who did not believe in predicting, and that this is natural instinct has been adjusted and integrated with long calculations. At the same time, I freed my soul, mind and heart of all care, solicitude and vexation. All of these prerequisites for presaging I achieved in part by means of the brazen tripod.

Nostradamus died in 1566, at the age of sixty-two. His prophecies, and the various interpretations that people continue to attribute to them, have survived for a great deal longer.

*****

Despite the warnings of his wife, Henry II decided to 'break another lance' with the captain of his Scottish guard, and when the lances did indeed break between them, a splinter somehow worked its way beneath the king's visor, pierced his eye, and from there began a brief but deadly journey towards his brain. He finally died on 10 July, with the entire French court coming and going from his bedside, although Catherine de Medici was quick to prohibit visits by his mistress, the eternally young Diane de Poiters.

On Henry's death, little Francois became Francis II, and Mary Queen of Scots gained her second crown as she became the queen of France. When Francois was crowned at Rheims, Mary again broke with conventional fashions by wearing what was fast becoming her signature white: 'Her choice of colour sparked something of a controversy. Mary wore white to be different. She was asserting her flair for the theatrical, a prospect made all the more attractive by the fact she knew the colour suited her better. And the people loved her for it, nicknaming her "the white Queen" as a result' (Guy, 2009, p103). It is worth pointing out that Mary Queen of Scots as 'the white Queen' is in no way related to *The White Queen* saga as penned by the historical novelist Philippa Gregory.

Jousting accidents were certainly not uncommon, although actual fatalities on the field were relatively rare. Maimings, for the most part, did however occur on a semi-regular basis. Henry VIII suffered several serious falls during the times when he was able to enjoy the sport, one of which caused the wound in his leg, a serious injury that was then reopened during a second fall later on. This wound was in some sense partially responsible for the marked personality change in him, dovetailing with the death of his second wife Anne Boleyn. Pain management was pitifully inadequate in Tudor times, so any ongoing injury could quite understandably leave the attendant personality considerably frayed.

Given that he had, during his jousting days, just one living child (and a girl, at that) Henry's courtiers were forever fretting about what would happen to him were he to suffer just the sort of jousting accident that he eventually did. This was one of the reasons his father kept him so wrapped up in cotton wool during the period after his brother Arthur's death, and before he himself died and Henry then became king. There has also been speculation on whether Henry actually suffered some sort of concussive brain damage during the fall of 1536, which may have led to personality changes alongside the resultant wound in the leg and the aforementioned lack of adequate pain management. Personally, it seems more likely that social pressures had simply reached boiling point in his quest to sire a male child to carry on the dynasty.

It actually took a man of some remarkable nerve to mount a horse that was prepared in a silvery carapace all of its own, and ready to take to the tiltyard. Any potential jouster would need to possess considerable upper body strength, and considerable nerve also to then to actually wield the lance, racing down one side of said tiltyard with the express intent of unhorsing his opponent, who was busily coming at him at an incredible speed from the opposite direction but with precisely the same intent. Marks were awarded during the jousting match for the various points on the body at which the lance might strike if a complete unhorsing was unsuccessful, with bruising and fractures a common by-product of such a brutal sport. Sir Francis Bryan, a diplomat and distant Boleyn relation who served in the court of Henry VIII, lost an eye during a jousting match and thus wore an eyepatch for the rest of his life.

Chapter 28

The Rough Wooings of Mary Queen of Scots

Long before she became the teen queen of France, Mary Stuart was simply queen of Scotland, declared as such from the time when she was barely a week old, her father James V having died, apparently, from the dual disappointment of a crushing English defeat and also the patriarchal disappointment at having fathered a girl after his two sons perished in infancy. In England, Henry VIII soon set his sights on Mary as a potential bride for his son Edward, the future Edward VI, but the Scots, after initially accepting the corpulent king's 'kindly' offer, soon withdrew, breaking the terms of the treaty in the process. They sent Mary into hiding in various different locations, including a short stint on the romantic little island of Inchmahome, near Aberfoyle. Like a foiled, spoilt child, Henry VIII retaliated against the Scots with barely suppressed savagery, sending north forces led by Edward Seymour, uncle to young Edward, to teach the Scots a fearful bloody lesson in what it meant to turn down some Tudor goodwill.

In fact, things hadn't been well between England and Scotland for centuries. Matters certainly weren't helped when James V had stood his uncle Henry up, this snub arriving after at a proposed meeting during Henry's progress north in 1541. Mary Queen of Scots' mother, Mary of Guise – once mooted as a prospective fourth wife for Henry VIII – played the English at a stalling game as best as she could when the Tudor king offered his son as a suitor for her daughter, but in the end the Scots were forced to take drastic measures in order to stop the vicious attacks that Edward Seymour and his army were orchestrating on their country. Even Edinburgh itself was besieged, but the castle held out against the invading English forces, although Holyrood Abbey was sacked and the remains of those interred there were desecrated, the bones scattered far and wide, some of them never to be recovered.

Things came to a head between the two warring countries with the Battle of Pinkie Cleugh, near Musselburgh, in 1547, a defeat for the Scots that was so devastating that the choice was made soon after to send the young Mary to France for her own safety, securing her to the bosom of her mother's Guise family and thus the royal court as well. Meanwhile, whole areas of Scotland were razed to the ground by the English forces, with entire villages, lands and livelihoods laid to waste. Among Henry VIII's orders on the initial campaigns had been the chilling line exhorting his troops not to leave 'one stone standing atop another', and also that not one person was to be spared the sword, not even women or children. However, with the treaty that existed with France, support was sent to Scotland by the French court to help repel the English invaders: 'This, of course, would mean a permanent French presence in Scotland but, in the circumstances, the terms of the Treaty of Haddington were pronounced "verray ressonabill"' (Plowden, 2010, p25). Eventually, the whole sorry affair was sorted out by the treaty of Boulogne in 1549. Mary Queen of Scots sailed for France from Dumbarton Castle with an entourage that included the famous 'Four Maries' of legend, Mary Beaton, Mary Seton, Mary Fleming, and Mary Livingston, all of them the children of various Scots nobles or ladies-in-waiting who were around the young queen's age.

Considering what was to come, it is no exaggeration to say that her years in France were to be among the happiest of Mary's tumultuous life. While her daughter sailed off toward her new life, Mary of Guise became regent of Scotland, ruling the fractured country for her daughter while Mary enjoyed that aforementioned carefree childhood in France, well away from the clutches of the grasping Henry VIII and his dynastic pretensions. However, when Mary eventually returned to Scotland, the clashes with England – particularly between the personalities of the-then ruling queens – soon came to the fore, with cataclysmic consequences.

Chapter 29

The Curious, Creepy Life of Catherine de Medici

Catherine de Medici, alongside Elizabeth I and Mary Queen of Scots, made up the triumvirate of fascinating sixteenth-century female rulers, although chronologically Catherine came first. She was married to Henry, Duke of Orleans, the future Henry II of France, on 28 October 1533, when she was just fifteen years old; Elizabeth Tudor was just a newborn at the time, and Mary Queen of Scots wasn't even a glimmer in her father's patriarchal eyes. Catherine de Medici was also from far humbler beginnings than either Elizabeth or Mary, at least in one sense – the Italian Medicis were bankers and not royalty, although the distinction has become slightly blurred in more modern times – but she was also the Pope's niece, which served to give her a considerable amount of kudos in the marriage market.

The marriage between Catherine and Henry was far from a love match, with Henry busily besotted by his mistress Diane de Poiters, which left Catherine neglected and shunted into the background as a result. To make matters worse, the marriage went on for ten years without there being any sign of Catherine producing any children, despite Diane encouraging Henry in this department as best she could. Catherine herself resorted to ever more desperate measures in order to conceive a royal heir, consulting astrologers – she was a famous patron of the practice, most notably with Nostradamus – and as a result she took potions and pills in astonishing amounts, including on one occasion drinking the urine of a mule in order to increase her chances of conceiving. It has been suggested that some of these 'remedies' may have contributed to the ill-health and less than stable psychological dispositions of her many children. Another theory has it that there was some 'problem' either with her sexual organs or with those of her husband – a possible penile deformity – and that all that was required to remedy the fact was some undisclosed advice from an attendant physician. Either way, once Catherine began producing heirs to the French throne she didn't stop until she had sired an astonishing ten children, eight of whom survived the high infant mortality rate of the times. Her first child was Francis, followed by Elisabeth and then Claude, Louis and Charles, and then Henry, Margaret and Hercules, and then finally Victoria and Joan. Victoria and Joan were twins, and during their birth Catherine almost died. After this, the doctors advised that she and her husband cease from producing any further children. Joan was stillborn, and Victoria died a little over a month and a half later.

Although superficially Catherine and Diane de Poiters coexisted at the French court on fairly peaceful terms, tensions behind closed doors remained high between the two women until Henry's death from the jousting accident already described in a previous chapter. At this point Catherine pulled her considerable rank, and Diane was effectively expelled from court and given a second-rate chateau to shut her up. In the previous years leading up to this event, it was said that Catherine had a hole drilled in the floor of her bedroom, directly above the bedroom that the king shared with Diane, and that she used to spy on the couple when they were making love. Other rumours said that Catherine was actually a witch and that she used spells and potions for matters other than the conceiving of children; also that she consulted all manner of astrologers, among them the aforementioned Nostradamus, and that she lived her life rigidly by their predictions. It was said that Catherine carried with her a talisman made by Nostradamus, an item concocted of various metals mixed in with the blood of a human and a goat. Viewing things from a purely patriarchal point of view – this was, after all, the lens through which the world was seen back then – Catherine was 'doomed' from the start, given the time it took her to produce a child. Witches were said to be the very antithesis of fecundity, so the delay she had in getting pregnant was pretty much the legacy she was left carrying even after she did finally conceive.

Besides Nostradamus, Catherine also consulted an occultist called Cosimo Ruggeri, a far more elusive figure, who was said to be both a witch and a sorcerer besides being also a simple astrologer. Cosimo seems to have come into the ascendancy after the death of Nostradamus in 1566. He is said to have told Catherine, quite correctly, that three of her sons would become kings, this with the help of an enchanted mirror. Cosimo Ruggeri also predicted that Catherine would die near St Germain.

Such was her belief in his predictions that she abandoned the building of a palace in the diocese of St Germain, near the Louvre. However, when Catherine eventually died in 1589 in Blois, the name of the priest who delivered the last rites was … Julien de St Germain. Certainly, Catherine's posthumous reputation hasn't been helped by the likes of *La Reine Margot*, the 1845 novel by Alexandre Dumas, centring around Catherine's involvement in the 1572 Massacre of St Bartholomew's Eve. The novel has also been adapted into a movie, in which Catherine was played by Italian actress Virna Lisi.

Besides being snubbed in favour of Diane de Poitiers, Catherine was also briefly eclipsed by her daughter-in-law, Mary Queen of Scots, when Henry and Catherine's first-born son, Francois, ascended to the throne. However, on his untimely death, Catherine quickly saw that Mary was sent packing back to Scotland, ostensibly in order to keep an eye on the Catholic situation over there. Legend has it that the two women had never seen eye-to-eye from the moment they first met, with Mary apparently pulling rank as queen of Scotland only to have Catherine pull considerably more rank over her as queen of France. The fact that Mary was later apparently heard referring to Catherine as a 'merchant's daughter' didn't help matters much, although this wouldn't be the last time that a wry comment from the Scots queen would land her in trouble at a later date (Robert Dudley and Elizabeth Tudor).

After the death of Francis II and the departure of Mary Queen of Scots, Catherine de Medici effectively ruled France while her son Charles was crowned as Charles IX. He was only nine years old at the time and apparently cried at his coronation. He had also developed something of a crush on Mary Queen of Scots and there was briefly talk that she might stay in France and marry him after the death of Francis, but there was no way Catherine would continue to allow Mary to live in her royal household now that the moment had come when she could finally get rid of her.

France was by this time in the grip of a series of religious wars that would dog it for decades, the absolute nadir being the aforementioned infamous Massacre of St Bartholomew's Eve, in August 1572. In the lead-up to this notorious nightmare, an abortive assassination attempt on Admiral Coligny – a Huguenot (Protestant) leader – caused Catherine to instigate a pre-emptive strike on his Huguenot compatriots before they rose in revenge for the attack. Although it was Charles IX who gave the order to kill the Huguenots, many historians believe that this was entirely at his mother's instigation, and such an act ensured her a prime place in the annals of historical infamy. The slaughter that followed on the streets of Paris soon spread throughout France, with thousands of Huguenot men, women and children being killed by Catholics from all walks of life: 'Private vendettas as well as religious hatred culminated in vandalism, barbarism and murder so that Paris, said one shocked observer, "was like a conquered city", and the Seine ran red with blood. Killing and butchery spilled over into the provinces, bringing the grisly total of deaths to ten thousand: one thousand at Orleans, eight hundred at Lyons and possibly four thousand in Paris' (Baldwin Smith, 1969, p147). It turned out that the Pope was so pleased with the proceedings that he had a medal struck especially for the occasion. It may be that as many as 70,000 Protestants were killed in all, but exact figures are hard, if not impossible to come by.

Just before Charles IX died at the age of just twenty-three, he named his mother as regent in his wake. His brother Henry, next in line to the throne, was currently the newly elected king of the Polish-Lithuanian Commonwealth. However, it wasn't long before Henry returned to France to take up the mantle of kingship, although throughout his reign he relied heavily on the advice and experience of his mother in regard to all matters of state. It was during this time that Catherine became something of a peacemaker, travelling widely around France in an attempt to make peace between the Catholics and the Huguenots. Despite this, her reputation still remains that of the consummate political poisoner, the tarnish so complete that she was once even cast as the main menace in a 1960s *Doctor Who* serial (now lost), not to mention being the foil for Mary Queen of Scots in the *Reign* TV series, where she was played with scenery-chewing relish by Megan Follows.

Chapter 30

Francis II and His Frightful Ear: Abscesses in Tudor Times

Francis II didn't have the best start in life. The first-born of Catherine de Medici and Henry II of France, he suffered from continual health problems throughout his young life, most probably because of all the strange potions and remedies that his mother had ingested in her attempt to fulfil her duty as a royal broodmare. For starters, Francis was short, and had a stutter; his nose often ran, and he suffered flushes and melancholy periods of mood that might last for days, if not weeks on end. He was in fact the polar opposite to his Amazonian, high-spirited child bride-to-be, Mary Queen of Scots.

When he became king of France on the death of his father in a jousting accident it was actually Mary's uncles, the Duke of Guise and the Cardinal of Lorraine, who really ran things, shunting his mother, Catherine de Medici, into the background and rendering the new king and queen as little more than a pair of political puppets. To be fair, Francis and Mary were little more than children at the time, having not expected to take up the reins of power for some considerable time.

In the months that followed their succession to the throne of France, Francis and Mary were, among other things, powerless spectators to the brutal reprisals that followed the discovery of the Amboise conspiracy, wherein countless Huguenot rebels were slaughtered before the palace of Amboise, some of them sewn into sacks and then thrown into the river and drowned in order to save time (it seems that even the sixteenth-century appetite for inventive cruelty and slaughter could find things a little tedious and time-consuming at times). Other victims were hung on the battlements before the windows of the palace so that the royal parties were able to witness their death-throes at close quarters, while taking a little wine and some nibbles. Such is the romantic aura that surrounds Mary Stuart that the Austrian biographer Stefan Zweig attempted to paint even this sorry episode in her life in a polished light: 'Now she watched the awesome sight of a human being, hands tied behind the back, kneeling with head on the block and awaiting the fall of the executioner's axe. She heard for the first time the curiously muffled and dull tone of steel that severs living flesh, she saw the blood squirt, and the head rolling away from the body into the sand' (Zweig, 2011, p46). As a result of these vicious reprisals and the other rumours about his ill-health, the common folk of France developed an almost irrational loathing of Francis, their sickly young king. They said that he drank the blood of babies in order to survive, and that his mother was a sorceress (see the previous chapter) who had employed poison to pave her husband's path to the throne.

In late November 1560 Francis developed what at first appeared to be a simple ear infection. However, an abscess soon developed and it became clear that without urgent assistance he would die. It was suggested that performing a partial lobotomy – a trepanation – might help alleviate his condition, but Catherine de Medici was horrified by the suggestion, and openly baulked at the idea of a king of France walking around with half of his brain missing. A trepanation involves a hole being drilled into the skull at the point required, the procedure being so old by the time it was suggested to Francis (there are prehistoric skulls with trepanation holes) that it may not have been so outlandish. That said, the scanty documentation that survives in regard to their earlier attempts relates to the fact that a hole in the head was drilled in order to release the evil spirits said to be lurking within, so it wasn't quite the ideal treatment from a medically sound point of view. Such a delicate operation of course carried great risk to the patient, with the possibility of brain damage being the most obvious, alongside blood loss and of course the constant possibility of infection.

In the event, poor Francis died on 5 December of that year, and Catherine de Medici became regent of France while her nine-year-old son Charles was crowned as the next king, Charles IX. In Scotland, the outspoken Protestant preacher John Knox said that Francis had died because his ear, being a Catholic ear, would not hear the truthful word of God and had become diseased as a result of such disobedience. Knox had been similarly spiteful to Mary Queen of Scots' mother, Mary of Guise, when she had died of dropsy while holed up in Edinburgh Castle, trying desperately to hold the country stable for her daughter. The flesh of her legs had been so soft and swollen that it was said that one could stick their fingers into it as though it were a warm slab of butter.

As a result of her husband's death, Mary Queen of Scots entered into the traditional forty days of mourning customary for a French queen, shutting herself up in a darkened room and for the most part receiving only visits from close royal friends and a few of the more concerned ambassadors. It was during this period that the famous '*deuil blanc*' portrait of Mary was painted, where she is wearing her signature white in the correct context of the French court at the time, as a sign of mourning.

Chapter 31

Mean Queen Liz: A Beginner's Guide to Bear-Baiting

Bear-baiting, whereby a chained, or sometimes a loose, bear is harassed, then attacked and then killed by dogs, was a popular 'sport' in Tudor times, and was in fact said to have been perhaps Elizabeth I's favourite 'pastime'. She liked the spectacle of bear-baiting so much that when there was a motion to ban it on Sundays she had the suggestion rapidly overruled. The Elizabethan chronicler Robert Laneham described one such bear-baiting that Elizabeth might have witnessed as follows:

> it was a sport very pleasant to see, to see the bear, with his pink eyes, tearing after his enemies approach; the nimbleness and wait of the dog to take his advantage and the force and experience of the bear again to avoid his assaults; if he were bitten in one place how he would pinch in another to get free; that if he were taken once, then by what shift with biting, with clawing, with roaring, with tossing and tumbling he would work and wind himself from them; and when he was loose to shake his ears twice or thrice with the blood and the slaver hanging about his physiognomy.

As one of Elizabeth's biographers, Anne Somerset, put it: 'Such cruel spectacles were an unattractive feature of the age, and Elizabeth was typical of her countrymen in seeing nothing wrong with them. The sufferings of the animals involved were looked on as highly comical' (Somerset, 1997, p469).

These 'entertainments' took place in specially constructed 'bear gardens' that were scattered throughout the capital and indeed around the country. A set of famous bear gardens were located at Southwark, at the notorious area known as Paris Gardens, which also housed a sizeable number of brothels. A stand collapsed at Paris Gardens in 1583 during a bear-baiting and several people were killed during the melee. The puritans jumped on this as a reason to suggest banning the sport on a Sunday, but this was more to do with their strict religious observances than for any concern with the cruelty to the poor bears themselves.

As well as bears being baited for sport, bulls and horses were also exposed to torment for the amusement of the masses, and sometimes animals other than hounds were used to attack them. In the reign of James VI/I there is a record of a lion being pitted against a bear on one occasion, with bets of course being taken on the outcome. Bulls were used for baiting more often than bears because bears were far harder to come by, although bullfighting itself remained a singularly Spanish cruelty for centuries to come. As said, people often wagered large amounts of money on these contests and the bears that survived more than one fight against the attack dogs became famous. All of them, however, succumbed in the end. Wagers were laid depending on the likelihood of the bear surviving from one match to the next. An unchained bear stood a good chance of surviving, while a bear chained either by the neck or by the ankle was far more likely to succumb under the onslaught of the dogs.

Considering the scarcity of wild bears in England, it was actually in the interest of the owners that they survived these 'matches' and dogs were usually called off before the wretched animal was actually killed. The survivors of these brutal encounters soon became firm favourites with the general public, with names such as 'Ned Whiting', 'Blind Bess' and 'Harry Hunks', amongst others. One of the most famous was the bear called 'Sackerson', which was namechecked by Shakespeare in *The Merry Wives of Windsor*. Bear-baiting continued to draw in large crowds even as the theatre grew in popularity. After the death of Elizabeth I, her successor, James VI/I, was said to have been so enthused by the sight that he found a way to import polar bears to England in order to 'partake', as well as using the animals from the menagerie at the Tower of London.

Henry VIII's fourth wife, Anne of Cleves, was said to have been watching a bear-baiting from her window at Rochester when the king burst in on her in disguise, Henry determined that he should lay eyes on his potential bride for the first time before her official entry into London. Given the size and also the temperament of Henry Tudor, it must be wondered whether Anne thought that one of the poor creatures below had in fact escaped the spectacle and somehow found its way up to her apartments.

A sport that was far more common among the lower classes was cock-fighting, because cocks were cheaper and – like bulls – easier to come by. Henry VIII for one was actually a big fan of the sport: 'Henry attended the traditional cockfights, for which, in 1533-4, he built new cockpits at Greenwich and Whitehall, the latter being a curious octagonal structure with a lantern roof. Both had tiered rows of seating, with a special chair for the King and a viewing gallery for the Queen. The fighting birds were kept in nearby coops' (Weir, 2008, p111). The Earl of Shrewsbury, who was the main custodian of Mary Queen of Scots during her political imprisonment in England, had a cockpit close by to his main residence of Sheffield Castle, although there is no record of his charge 'enjoying' any bouts. Indiscreet she may have been, but Mary Queen of Scots seems not to have shared the bloodthirsty appetite of her English cousin.

The Tudors were as ingenious at devising new and nasty ways to kill animals as they were in slaughtering each other. Besides bears and cocks, one could also witness in the various cities of England rat-baiting, badger-baiting, dog fights, and even the public whipping of older, wounded bears no longer thought fit for the arena. Bull-baiting was somehow considered to be particularly good for tenderising the meat ahead of eventual human consumption. However, there were many critics of these blood sports even at the time, and several of the better-known bear pits were closed down by Oliver Cromwell during his brief reign. The bear pits, and various other arenas, were noisy, rowdy places, rife with pickpocketing and also prostitution, although as time went on the various owners devised new ways to make them somewhat more salubrious, including serving drinks and building special balconies upon which spectators might eat a meal as they watched the animal of their choice being torn to death. It took rather a long time for these blood sports to fall out of favour, and it is possible to see their remnants still in several of the street names in South London today, namely 'Bear Gardens' and 'Bear Lane'.

Besides the bear pits and the cockpits and all of the various other ways the Tudors devised to terrorise animals for their pleasure, they also hunted extensively, a 'tradition' still enjoyed by some members of today's royal family. Whereas nowadays it is the unfortunate fox that bears the brunt of this so-called 'sport', back in Tudor times it was the deer that was hounded almost to the point of extinction. Only the rich – the nobility, basically – were allowed to hunt deer, while the poor working classes had to make do with snaring hares and rabbits.

Henry VIII passed a law in 1532 stating that a certain number of animals needed to be slain because they were 'vermin'. In 1566 his daughter Elizabeth amended and added to the bill when she was queen. Basically, almost anything that wasn't human and couldn't be exploited in some way or another had a bounty on its head and was considered fair game. According to the conditions of the bill, various birds were worth a penny each, whereas a fox was worth up to twelve pence. Hedgehogs were also on the list, as were badgers, woodpeckers and kingfishers, among others. Hedgehogs were singled out because it was thought (yes, really) that they sucked the milk from cattle at night.

Henry VIII was said to have spent up to five hours a day – in his svelte prime, of course – in the saddle chasing deer, with his daughter Elizabeth also being an ardent hunter. One of the royal hunting grounds stretched over the entire area of what is now known as Hyde Park and also Kensington Gardens. Those who were not actually taking part in the hunt could watch from specially set up grandstand area, partaking in food and drink as they did so. When one tract of land had been exhausted of all living things, attention would turn to other available tracts of land. Henry VIII brought up/seized a large area near Marylebone from the Abbess of Barking. Ditches and ramparts were constructed around many of these hunting grounds, keeping the 'game' in and the poachers and the public – i.e., the lower classes – out. Horses used in the hunt were bred in much the same manner that they are today, the better to rear a stronger, more durable steed.

Despite the protests of a select few – Thomas More and the scholar Erasmus, for example – hunting was considered to be the proper pastime for a gentleman, to be valued and indulged above the need to read and write, or to do anything vaguely cerebral. Hawking, or falconry, was also considered a most excellent sport, whereby falcons, hawks and occasionally even eagles were trained up and then deployed in order to hunt small 'game' such as mice, voles and other, smaller birds. These hunting birds were trained by falconers, and the sport was prohibitively expensive. The birds needed time to be properly trained and were housed in special cages called 'mews'. They had to be taken from their nest at a very young age, the better to get them used to the company of humans.

Were this not bad enough, sometimes the birds were temporarily blinded, having their eyes sewn shut with a needle and thread. The end of the thread was then tied over and around the head of the bird so that the falconer might open and close the poor creature's eyes at will. Even more expensive were all of the paraphernalia the falconer would require, including specially designed leather gloves and wrist-straps, as well as bells for the ankles of the birds so that they might keep track of them at all times. Likewise, the hunters themselves liked to be kitted out in the latest fashions when they went hunting, and so accessorised wrist-straps were all the rage, alongside special riding outfits, saddles and so on and so forth.

Sometimes, the humans exploiting or abusing the animals would fall foul of them in rather gruesome fashion. Many people were injured after falling from their horses, sometimes being trampled in the process. In fact, it is estimated that one in ten fatal accidents in the sixteenth century involved an animal in one form or another, usually horses. The horse was the Tudor equivalent of a car, after all, so one need only do the equivalent maths to understand the relatively similar statistics involved. Many people were kicked by horses, including the unfortunate Anthony Coke, who was kicked rather badly by the courtier Thomas Heneage's horse as he rode into Lincoln, during August 1550. By all accounts Heneage's horse was a fine animal, said by the coroner's jury to be worth at least eight times more than May's mare.

Where a horse was involved, a cart was more often than not equally culpable, especially if you then added a hill or steep slope into the equation. A horse placed between the shafts of a cart in order to regulate the steering was called a 'thill horse', and a great many mishaps occurred when the poor beast lost control of the cargo; icy roads were a particular hazard in this regard. In a similar vein, cattle and oxen that were used to pull carts and steer ploughs on farms were also prone to causing rather gruesome accidents, with the various limbs of drivers or workers sometimes being lopped off in the process of reining them in.

Farms were often open-plan and easily accessible by the public, and as a result a passing stroll might end up with the walker being gored by a bull, or else trampled by spooked cattle. Pigs were also something a peril, but for the most it was boars – wild or otherwise – that were apt to gore passers-by with their horns. Given their timid nature, the statistics for people being done to death by a sheep were understandably low, but people did occasionally perish in such an innocuous fashion. Sheep taken down to fast-flowing rivers to be washed before they were to be sheared could become a lethal death-trap for the unwary. Those washing the sheep could become entangled in the wool and then unable to swim. Such an incident occurred on a ford on the Riven Avon in Wiltshire when four people died, apparently after going to the aid of a solitary farmworker.

Several centuries before Alfred Hitchcock brought the terror of *The Birds* to the big screen, birds were the causes of several mishaps, scarring and even deaths, although usually because of the backfiring of some endeavour to do away with them. For instance, in 1599 John Norton of Milton Regis in Kent accidentally shot himself in the chest while trying to hit a pigeon that he intended to use to feed his pet hawk. As he took aim from his window, a wire on the window frame tangled with the sear – the section of the lock that held the hammer ready to fire once the trigger was pulled – and he ended up with the aforementioned wound.

Of all the animals apt to cause peril for humanity, the deadliest was also the smallest: the common rat. Rats spread innumerable diseases to humans and could wipe out great swathes of the population, so sometimes quite extraordinary lengths were taken in order to exterminate them. Lethal poisons were deployed to get rid of rats and these were sometimes mistakenly eaten by children, or even mistaken by cooks for ingredients. Barbara Gilbert of Leicestershire poisoned herself when she mistook some arsenic trioxide (ratsbane) for flour and mixed it into the dish she was preparing, thereby falling ill. Whether she actually ingested some of the ratsbane or not is unclear, but if that had been the case then she would have almost certainly died.

Chapter 32

Stalking, Sixteenth Century Style: Mary Queen of Scots and the Case of Pierre Chastelard

On her return to Scotland from France, the newly widowed Mary Queen of Scots soon eclipsed her cousin Elizabeth I of England as the most eligible woman in all of Europe. She quickly received offers of blissful matrimony from all the great powers scattered across the Continent.

The front-runner for her hand in marriage was at one time Don Carlos, son of Phillip II, Elizabeth's former brother-in-law. Unfortunately, Don Carlos was deformed (his portraits do not seem to bear this out, however) and had shown signs of mental instability from a very young age. He tortured animals, particularly his horses, with the simple purpose of hearing them scream. On one occasion he is said to have purposely blinded every single horse in the royal stable. Besides that, he also enjoyed roasting various animals alive and then forcing servants to eat his sadistic concoctions. He was also in the habit of making a passing grab at any particular woman that took his fancy. In 1562, while he was pursuing a fleeing maid down a flight of stairs, he fell badly and received such a blow to the head that an operation was considered the only way of saving his life. Unfortunately, medical science being what it was back in Tudor times the operation only made him even more sadistic and erratic. One day, while walking beneath a window, he was accidentally splashed with water. His response was to order that the house be set on fire in order to punish the perpetrator. Such occurrences continued with ever-increasing frequency, to the point where his father was forced to have him locked up – sectioning, sixteenth-century style – and he died not long afterwards, apparently from natural causes, although there were rumours that he had been poisoned. Therefore, it seems that Mary Queen of Scots had a lucky escape from Don Carlos, the sort in which she specialised for much of her Scottish career, be it physical, fraternal or even matrimonial.

Being such a catch, it wasn't long before Mary soon picked up her very own stalker, again in a distinctly sixteenth-century style. His name was Pierre Chastelard, a French poet who had accompanied Mary on her return to Scotland in the wake of her widowhood and been much enamoured of her, or so the court gossips said. Not long after that he returned to Paris, but it wasn't long before he was back in Scotland again, simmering with desire for a queen who had partnered him in the dances at Holyrood Palace and who also had a habit of whispering sweet nothings in his ear as they capered around those halls and galleries, all in the platonic and proper fashion of courtly love, of course. However, it appeared that Chastelard was quite convinced that Mary was in fact madly in love with him and so he took it upon himself to hide under her bed or in her wardrobe – accounts differ for the first occasion – where he was eventually discovered by Mary's maids, although initially he was pardoned and things went on in pretty much the same fashion as they had before. It was then that Chastelard decided to hide under her bed a second time – on Valentine's Day, no less – on this occasion leaping out and grabbing the young queen in an embrace of fevered, frustrated passion as she prepared herself for bed. Her half-brother, the Earl of Moray, responded to her screams, but on arriving in the room he declined Mary's orders to run the presumptuous Chastelard through with his sword. The poet was instead executed according to the letter of the law at St Andrews, by the simple means of beheading. His last words to his beloved queen were apparently along the lines of 'Adieu! To the most beautiful and cruel princess in the world!' Mary herself was apparently a witness to the execution and fainted dead away at the sight.

It has since been speculated that Chastelard was in fact far from the ardent stalker that he first appeared to be. He may have been a Huguenot agent who had been sent to Scotland with the express order that he was to smear the spotless reputation of the Catholic queen of Scots in any way that might be deemed feasible. What also casts a shadow of some doubt and thus further scandal over the whole affair is that Mary apparently wanted him silenced immediately on the second occasion that he attempted to molest her, even ahead of his formal execution. It may have been that 'Mary knew she had overindulged his (Chastelard's) attendance and he misinterpreted the "familiar usage in a varlet" to the point of madness' (Graham, 2009, p168). As a result, she wanted quickly to cover the tracks of her folly, or even that she may have realised or been informed of the fact that he might be a Huguenot spy sent to entrap her, and wanted him silenced before any possible further damage to her reputation might have been wrought.

Chapter 33

The Degenerate Lord Darnley: Alcoholism in Tudor Times

When Mary Queen of Scots finally settled on the choice of her second husband she was unwittingly walking headlong into a series of disasters that would see her first lose her crown, then her liberty, and finally her life. But on the surface her choice of spouse, Henry, Lord Darnley, had it all going on, at least when she first laid eyes on him on home soil, in the grounds of Wemyss Castle in Scotland. He was tall, blond, boyishly pretty, fairly athletic, and, most importantly of all, he also came with a joint guarantee of being from prize Tudor and Stewart stock, being the son of Matthew Stewart 4th Earl of Lennox and Lady Margaret Douglas, the daughter of Margaret Tudor, one of Henry VIII's sisters (also Mary's grandmother). Darnley and Mary were, in fact, cousins, but the Pope was soon on hand to provide a dispensation for this bothersome little detail. Because of Darnley's rather dynamic credentials of descent, Elizabeth I vehemently opposed the marriage, but by that time Mary was tired of being told what to do by her cousin, and she and Darnley married anyway, tying the knot officially on 29 July 1565.

Prior to her courtship with Darnley, Mary had been kindly instructed on exactly who she should marry by her notorious spinster cousin, with the queen of England's favourite, Robert Dudley, dangled under her nose as a potential spouse on one occasion. Such a man, with his traitor's pedigree and his wife's unexplained death hanging over him, was so far beneath Mary's rank and consideration that her ambassadors were not entirely sure whether the entire suggestion was some sort of a joke. It wasn't. More than likely Elizabeth knew that the suggestion would receive a lukewarm welcome, but she and her councillors merely wanted to delay Mary as long as possible from perhaps entering into a marriage with a powerful Catholic prince, one who might encourage her to claim her legitimate right to the English throne by way of invasion. There is also the possibility that Elizabeth wanted Dudley to act as some sort of a spy at the Scottish court, but even so, the suggestion that she may have been serious where the proposal was concerned still leaves many historians agog.

It has been speculated that Elizabeth and indeed the entire English court knew full well what a degenerate Darnley was and deliberately allowed him to sally forth into Mary's arms, knowing that he would most likely bring disaster on Elizabeth's 'dear sister and cousin'. But little can be concretely proved in this direction either. Certainly, Mary's eternal nemesis, Sir William Cecil, may have had a hand in steering such a sour prize in her direction, given that he had dedicated the better part of his passions to bringing about her downfall, apparently by any means necessary. Darnley's mother, Margaret, was thrown into the Tower of London for a short stint by way of punishment for Mary and Darnley's disobedience, but even this wasn't enough to keep the courting couple from fast-tracking their romance to the altar at Holyrood.

Mary and her new husband enjoyed a few months of blissfully wedded life, but it wasn't long before Darnley began showing his true, despicable colours. Mary soon discovered that her new husband was petulant, irresponsible and immature, and prone to throwing the most enormous hissy fit whenever someone disagreed with him, or went against his wishes. On one occasion he got so drunk at a dinner party that he took to berating Mary before the other guests, to the point where she apparently fled the scene in tears. On this basis, Mary soon decided against granting him the crown matrimonial and therefore the full rights enjoyed as joint sovereign. She also had a special stamp made up that could be used in lieu of his signature, as he spent most of his time hunting, hawking, and leching in the taverns of Edinburgh, as opposed to attending to any of his royal duties. Darnley also began drinking heavily in public, and it was while frequenting the taverns and brothels of Edinburgh that he was reported apparently enjoying the company of male 'professionals' with almost as much frequency as he did that of the women. Whether or not he shared a bed with Mary's Italian secretary, David Rizzio, in anything other than a platonic sense is still open to debate, whatever may have been depicted in the latest Hollywood movie concerning Mary's life (2018). One particular anecdote about his degenerate ways has Darnley committing some obscene act on a golf course that was so utterly shocking and depraved to all those who knew of or witnessed it that to this day there is little idea as to what it actually was. The historian can once again merely speculate with a raised eyebrow and then merely marvel at his apparent ingenuity where a golf club is concerned. He was also less than an attentive husband to the queen, and when she 'fell ill during the autumn he did not sit at her bedside as she had sat at his, but continued "at his pastime". His companions were "gentlemen willing to satisfy his will and affections," who sycophantically listened to his grievances and led him astray, drinking and "vagadondizing" in disreputable parts of Edinburgh, to which he accompanied them with alacrity' (Bingham, 1995, p121).

There was no doubt that Darnley was putting Mary's reputation in grave danger by his behaviour, but he was also risking her life and her health with his wanton ways. Darnley was almost certainly syphilitic, which may have been merely one of the various maladies that he picked up from the prostitutes whose services he is said to have engaged. Mary had nursed him through one bout of something involving spots and sweating at Stirling Castle while they were still courting, and it was something short of a miracle that he didn't infect both her and their son, the future James VI/I, with a disease that would soon see him erupting in sores and then watching in horror as his nose first slowly disintegrated and then fell off altogether.

Syphilis remains one of the more 'notorious' sexually transmitted infections, with the signs and symptoms spreading over four distinct stages: primary, secondary, latent and then finally tertiary. In the primary stage, sores are the main obvious symptom; once the secondary stage is reached, a rash may occur, particularly prevalent on the palms of the hands and/or the soles of the feet. Strangely, the latent phase of syphilis sees all of these earlier symptoms disappear, said absence lasting for some several years or more. It has been speculated that Mary may have wed Darnley during the latent phase of his syphilis and thus may have been ignorant of the fact that he was thus infected, although, if this were indeed the case, then he may have gone into the marriage with the full knowledge that he had the disease. When the final, or tertiary, stage of syphilis occurs, small non-cancerous growths called 'gummas' may occur – anywhere on the body, by all accounts – alongside various neurological disorders and also heart problems.

By the time that his nose was collapsing, Darnley and Mary were completely estranged, and Darnley had little more than a few weeks left to live, although the manner of his death would not result from syphilis at all, but as a result of one of the most audacious murders ever executed on Scottish soil.

Chapter 34

The Diabolical Death of David Rizzio: Mob Violence in Tudor Times

As Mary Queen of Scots' second husband, the degenerate Lord Darnley, began to reveal his rather callous and covetous colours, the disillusioned queen turned ever increasingly to her private secretary, David Rizzio, for support, solace, and the odd midnight game of cards. David Rizzio had originally been picked out as a possible bass singer for Mary's depleted stock of musicians, but the canny Italian quickly ascended the greasy pole of royal favour and soon was enjoying the queen's innermost confidences, and, some rumoured, her sexual favours as well.

Contemporary descriptions have David Rizzio appearing to onlookers as an ugly, hunchbacked dwarf, so if that was the case it seems doubtful if Mary would have spared him so much as a second glance. However, the portrait hanging over the spot near where his body was dumped in Holyrood Palace after his brutal murder does seem a fair sight more pleasing, so it may be a safer bet to assume that the 'ugly' rumours may have stemmed more from disaffected Protestant Scots lords who didn't care greatly at having a little Italian Catholic lording it over them. Either way, it wasn't long before Mary's husband was nursing an intense slight to his manhood, and so, egged on by those self-same disaffected Protestant Scots lords, who were eager to overthrow the little Italian in order to further their own advancement and also to halt a possible return to the Catholic faith, a plot was hatched to do away with poor Rizzio.

On 9 March 1566 David Rizzio was dining with the queen and several others of her staff and household in the small supper room still extant in Mary's well-trodden chambers in Holyrood Palace. Anyone who has visited Holyrood Palace might only have marvelled at how so many people – including the impending assassins – might have squeezed into such a small space, although this author was told by one of the attendants on duty at the time that back in Mary's day the room was far bigger than it was now. Anyway, the supper party was interrupted by

Darnley – at this point he and Mary were all but estranged – and then by the even more disturbing vision of the rumoured warlock Lord Ruthven, dangerously ill and appearing before them like some sort of ghost in a full suit of armour. Ruthven demanded that David Rizzio come out of the small supper room to answer the accusations made against him, particularly those pertaining to the queen's honour. While Darnley sat beside Mary and gently restrained her, Rizzio tried to hide, first in a corner and then by clinging to the skirts of the queen, who at the time was six months pregnant with the future James VI/I. Part of the murder plot may have involved causing Mary to miscarry with the shock, so that Darnley could then seize the reins of power for himself, at which point said reins would be promptly seized from his own incompetent hands by the Protestant lords, who saw themselves as infinitely more entitled to rule Scotland than some effete English upstart.

However, Mary was made of sterner stuff then they had ever imagined and didn't miscarry her child, although she was unable to prevent Rizzio from being plucked forth from the supper room, with blades flashing around her and 'at the same time, Ruthven's nephew, Kerr of Fawdonside, held his pistol so close to her that it rubbed up against her stomach, as he bent Rizzio's fingers back grimly, "so that for pain he was forced to forgo his grip"' (Tweedie, 2006, p142). The table in the supper room was overturned in the struggle and only the quick thinking of her half-sister, the Countess of Argyll, stopped the candles atop it from igniting the nearby tapestries and causing an even bigger calamity. Meanwhile, David Rizzio was dragged through the queen's bedroom and either there or in the audience chamber beyond he was stabbed by the various assassins a total of fifty-six times, his body then thrown down the nearby staircase. Today, a faux bloodstain is painted in by staff at Holyrood Palace near the aforementioned portrait of Rizzio to help the morbidly minded visitor discern the exact spot where David's body was first left before it was slung down the stairs, then to be stripped of all its clothes and belongings by a greedy porter who happened to be hovering nearby. It was said that the porter remarked that Rizzio's body – which had landed on some sort of chest – had returned to the place where it had originally lain, given that he had taken to sleeping on said chest in his early days at Holyrood in lieu of being assigned proper quarters.

Today, David Rizzio is believed to be buried in the churchyard of the Canongate Kirkyard on Edinburgh's Royal Mile – the grave is to the right of the entrance and is quite clearly marked – but it is far more likely that his corpse actually lies in an unmarked grave somewhere in the grounds of Holyrood Palace, close to the ruined abbey where it was said he was initially laid to rest.

In the wake of Rizzio's death Mary was herself held prisoner in Holyrood Palace while her rebellious nobles decided quite how they were to proceed with their plans. When she attempted to call for help from the window to the citizens of Edinburgh she was pulled back inside by her captors and told that she would be cut up into little pieces if she tried anything like it again. Still, she kept her cool and managed to get letters smuggled out to her supporters, while she herself did her best to win her treacherous husband over, convincing him that once the rebellious Protestant lords had what they wanted that they would dispose of him as deftly as they had poor David Rizzio. Mary was so convincing that Darnley was dumbstruck with fear at being double-crossed, and a day or so after Rizzio's murder they snuck out of Holyrood Palace in the dead of night to find horses and help waiting for them. During their flight legend has it that they stumbled over the freshly dug grave of poor Rizzio, at which point Mary is supposed to have muttered a veiled threat of revenge on those who had slain her secretary, with her husband at the top of the potential hit-list.

Mary managed to make the journey on horseback away from Edinburgh and over twenty-five gruelling miles to the safety of Dunbar Castle, stopping only to be sick because of her advanced pregnancy. At the same time she had to contend with Darnley trying to urge her horse on faster so that they could better outrun any potential pursuers. As always he was more concerned with his own safety than with his wife's, and callously commented that if Mary miscarried then they could easily make another child later on.

Mary had sworn that she would be avenge the murder of her secretary. Revenge, when indeed it came, would be explosive, to say the least.

Chapter 35

Smallpox: The Scarring of the Queen's Complexion

While the Sweating Sickness was perhaps the most feared of all of the terrible Tudor diseases, there was another malady that struck fear not only because of the threat to life but because the fate of the victim's face was often left hanging in the balance as well.

Among the many who contracted smallpox some of them remained scarred for life, even if they survived the actual disease itself. One of the main symptoms included blisters that broke out all over the body, and during Tudor times this seems also to have been accompanied by chills and a fever which would leave the patient bedridden and hovering on the brink of death for days at a time. When these blisters receded, or popped, they left often permanent scarring and could in some cases be so severe that they left the sufferer almost blind. Smallpox has been recorded as far back as 1,500BC, and in 1980 the World Health Organisation declared the global eradication of the disease.

Elizabeth I contracted smallpox on or around 10 October 1562. She was at Hampton Court Palace at the time and thought at first that she had merely caught a particularly bad cold; the chills and the fever were easily mistaken for various other maladies, after all. She took to her bed but her condition soon worsened and it became clear that she did in fact have smallpox. The country – and beyond, for she had many enemies and few friends – waited with bated breath to see if she would recover. For a while she hovered somewhere between life and death, totally delirious: 'After a week of violent fever all hope for her seemed gone. The queen was not expected to live and the court was in turmoil. In the midst of all the anxieties over English intervention in a French war of religion, there was this very real fear that Elizabeth would die. And die without having named an heir' (Dunn, 2004, p243). When she eventually did recover, her distressed ministers pressed on her more urgently than ever the need to marry and to provide the country with an heir – preferably male – something which she still steadfastly refused to do. The loyal Lady Mary Sidney – sister to the queen's favourite, Robert Dudley – had nursed her throughout the illness and then went on to catch the dreaded smallpox herself. While Elizabeth escaped with her famous alabaster complexion relatively unscarred, the unfortunate Lady Mary was left so disfigured by the ravages of the disease that she never returned to court again, except on the odd occasion when she would be allowed to visit the queen in secret, and with her face quite discreetly masked.

Mary Queen of Scots also contracted smallpox at some point during her long stay in France, but her complexion was saved far more completely than that of Elizabeth's, with the help of one of her physicians. Mary marvelled at the man's medical prowess in a letter to her 'dear cousin' after Elizabeth's own battle with the disease, but declined to pass on exactly what the all-important cure against permanent pits and scarring actually was.

Whatever the degree of actual smallpox scarring that she may or may not have suffered, the fact remained that over the years – and in a never-ending attempt to stave off the ravages of time – Elizabeth Tudor would submit her skin to rigours that would have actually put the highly infectious disease to shame. Dark or suntanned skin was a serious social no-no in Tudor times. It was a sign that you were perhaps a poor labourer, someone who spent far too much time outdoors, and thus various methods were employed in order to lighten the complexion and adopt a more 'aristocratic' air. A combination of lead and vinegar were sometimes used to lighten the skin, although the far more lethal combination of ceruse and white lead mixed together was said to yield better results, at least in the short term. The trouble was that this particular concoction was rarely washed off before being readministered rather vigorously. As a result a great many women perished from lead poisoning. The symptoms of lead poisoning were particularly unpleasant. As well as joint and muscle pain, a gradual loss of concentration was then followed on by more pronounced mood changes. It's not entirely impossible to imagine that some of Elizabeth's later irascibilities may have had less to do with the genes inherited from her father than from the fact that her system was in fact rather clogged up with this particular poisonous concoction. Damage to the kidneys and also the nervous system may also then occur, followed by seizures and possibly death.

As she grew older, Elizabeth is known to have used beeswax as a lotion and egg whites almost as a primer, to ensure that her elaborate make-up did not crack or fade. Sometimes, veins were traced out upon the forehead or neck in order to further imply the illusion of a healthy, vibrant complexion. For those unable – or indeed unwilling – to resort to some of the more extreme measures required in order to emulate that perfect alabaster complexion, there was always recourse to washing one's face either with a serving of cheap wine or even in a generous helping of their own urine. Another method involved a modest amount of bloodletting in order to literally drain the skin to the required pallor.

Elizabethan beauty standards required an emphasis on the eyes that led to overt eyebrow plucking. Many of the surviving portraits of the queen attest to this enthusiastic application of the tweezers, as they do to Elizabeth's somewhat elevated forehead. A high forehead was a sign of elegant stateliness, and several waves of hair might also fall prey to the tweezers in order to achieve this particular aesthetic ideal. Likewise, blushed or heavily rouged cheeks were seen as the ideal accompaniment to the overly pale complexion, achieved either through the use of dye or simply by pinching the flesh until it reddened under the resultant epidermal distress. Pale lips were remedied by using a variety of means, including egg whites and cochineal. Belladonna drops were sometimes used in order to make dull, tired eyes sparkle and making the pupils dilate; the chemicals in the plant served to block the receptors that make the pupils contract. However, it also has the adverse effect of causing visual distortions and occasionally even blindness among users.

Chapter 36

The Calamity at Kirk O'Field:
Political Assassinations

In Edinburgh, after the death of David Rizzio and the birth of the future James VI/I, Lord Darnley's popularity rapidly plummeted to a new low. Mary Queen of Scots was under no illusions about the fact that her husband had been a partial instigator of the plot to do away with poor Rizzio, and thus Darnley was forced to slink away to his father's stronghold of Glasgow, where the more obvious stages of syphilis soon began to overwhelm him. It wasn't long before he was bedridden and wearing a white taffeta mask over his face to hide the fact that his skin was erupting in blisters and his nose was all but falling off.

The main treatment for syphilis in Tudor times was mercury, which had the added unpleasant side effect of making the gums shrink and the teeth fall out, and therefore the production of saliva increased significantly as a result. To say that the formerly handsome, athletic Lord Darnley was no longer a pretty sight was something of an understatement. Besides the use of mercury, patients were also given rather vigorous 'sweat baths', as it was thought that intense perspiration might somehow remove the infection from the body by literally purging it via the pores of the afflicted. Elements of the guaiacum tree were also used in the treatment of syphilis, used both as a balm to dress the various skin eruptions and also as an oral tonic that might be taken by the patient at various points throughout the day. Mercury, however, remained the more preferred but also the more invasive treatment – it was sometimes administered rather painfully via the urethra – but the high toxicity meant that a great many patients succumbed to its effects before they actually died of syphilis itself. Sometimes the mercury was used simply as a balm, or else the patient was encouraged to inhale the fumes, usually in a sealed room with a large fire burning nearby, which encouraged perspiration, taking us back to the idea that excess sweating would somehow purge the body of the affliction. Such treatments might be carried out over weeks, if not months, at a time. As in the case of beauty balms, too much mercury could also cause kidney failure, besides the other various detrimental effects. The sheer length of the treatment with mercury gave rise to the saying, 'A night with Venus and a lifetime with Mercury.'

The series of events that began with Mary Queen of Scots travelling to Glasgow to fetch her husband home – ostensibly with a view to caring for his failing health – and which in fact ended in his brutal murder shortly after, have divided and baffled historians ever since. But these events form the very core of the concept of Mary Queen of Scots as either an impassioned, foolish, and naïve but ultimately innocent woman, or Mary Queen of Scots as a conniving and murderous adulteress, one who lured her husband to his death in the full, or at least partial knowledge of what was to befall him when they returned to Edinburgh.

Mary actually spent several days with Darnley in Glasgow, ostensibly on 'enemy territory', before she was able to convince him that it was safe to return to Edinburgh, this despite the fact that she had since pardoned several of the other plotters involved in the murder of Rizzio (since which time they had been flocking back to Scotland in their droves, many of them with a score to settle). None of these men were particularly renowned for their forgiving natures, and they were unlikely to have discounted the fact that Darnley had fled from their midst during the brief coup at Holyrood after Rizzio's murder, helping his wife to escape in the process.

Ahead of Mary's peace-making trip to Glasgow, a meeting had been convened at one of the queen's favourite castles, Craigmillar (not far at all from Holyrood itself), with Mary's council thrashing out as best they could the possible solutions to the ongoing 'Darnley dilemma'. Those historians partisan to Mary claim that she wasn't present during the meetings and that when she was confronted with the options she told her council firmly that she wanted nothing done that might besmirch her honour, or indeed anything that might jeopardise her son's right to succeed her. A second meeting was held shortly after at a different location, at which the queen was most definitely not present. It was here, so it seems, that the more solid idea of assassinating Darnley – rather than simply imprisoning or exiling him – was finally settled upon. Who precisely was present at these various meetings, and who said and suggested what, is also a matter of such conjecture that to list the 'suspects' here would risk elongating the chapter by some several pages or so.

On being brought back from Glasgow, Darnley was initially to convalesce at Holyrood Palace itself, before a house in Edinburgh called Kirk O'Field was suggested and then rather rapidly settled upon. Kirk O'Field lay not far from Holyrood Palace, on the site of what is now the University of Edinburgh (there is a Tesco Express almost directly opposite, for those having difficulty in discerning the exact location where his strangled body was later discovered). The adjacent side road, South College Street, is also a possibility for the discovery of both his and his unfortunate manservant's bodies.

As Darnley was universally despised by the nobility of Scotland, it was actually more of a question of who *wasn't* involved in his murder as opposed to who was. All that can be definitely discerned is that the cellars of the house at Kirk O'Field were at some point, not long after his arrival, packed with gunpowder, and that early in the hours of 10 February 1567 the whole place went up in flames, rousing almost the whole city with the explosion. Later on, nearby residents were to claim that they had borne witness to several bands of rather menacing looking men moving about the house in the dead of night, but no particular person was ever identified. Mary herself had been due to sleep in the house alongside her husband on that very night, but had 'conveniently' rushed off to attend a wedding masque down at Holyrood in the hours beforehand. As said, depending on which way one views the various conspiracy theories, Mary was either in it up to her neck and making sure that she was well clear of the fireworks, or else she was just damned lucky to have a prior engagement on the night the house was due to be 'demolished'.

Before the conflagration, Darnley, his manservant and various members of staff were alerted by the sounds of those several different bands of conspirators surrounding the house and were actually able to make a hasty escape through one of the windows, but they were caught and strangled or suffocated in the nearby garden. A drawing of the aftermath of the explosion was made by one of William Cecil's spies, but as a piece of accurate journalism it falls far short of the mark. The dimensions are all out of proportion and it puts one rather more in mind of the centrespread in an American comic book than of a serious historical document. In the drawing, both Darnley and his manservant are depicted as being partially clad, while nearby his son James sits up in his cradle and appears to be saying, 'Judge and avenge my cause, O Lord.'

It has to be said that murdering Darnley by attempting to blow him up with gunpowder had to be one of the most ham-fisted assassination attempts ever undertaken. Despite having been in circulation for some several hundred years in most of Europe as a weapon of war, gunpowder was still notoriously unstable and unreliable; rather like Darnley himself, by all accounts. By the fourteenth century, gunpowder was being made in large quantities in England. There was even a 'powder house' at the Tower of London by the middle of the fifteenth century. By the time of Darnley's assassination, gunpowder was made and stored at most of the castles and fortifications around the country. The gunpowder used at Kirk O'Field almost certainly came from the North Sea fortress of Dunbar Castle, property of the Earl of Bothwell.

Undoubtedly, the chief suspect in the assassination of Darnley was the aforementioned Earl of Bothwell, the swaggering macho borderer who was rising fast in Mary's favour at a time when she was becoming more and more politically isolated. Bothwell had helped Mary to regain control of Edinburgh after the death of David Rizzio. Later, when he had been wounded in a border skirmish with a notorious brigand, Mary had ridden a considerable distance over treacherous terrain to visit him in his fortress of Hermitage Castle (such a mercy dash served only to cement the idea that she was an adulteress in the eyes of her enemies, several months down the line). Bothwell had a track record of being steadfastly loyal to the crown even though the queen was Catholic and he was a Protestant. He was also a womaniser and a devout warrior, with a tinderbox of a temper and a tendency to resort to whatever means might be necessary in order to get his way.

On hearing the news of Darnley's untimely death, Elizabeth I urged her cousin to take swift action, as did the various other European powers: 'As for Mary, her reactions to the explosion and murder suggest her complete ignorance. Her astonishment and fear seem genuine; she acted as though she honestly believed that she, as well as Henry, was the intended victim of the gunpowder plot' (Doran, 2007, p107). However, instead of having Bothwell arrested and made a swift example of, Mary went ahead and married him instead. The story of quite *how* she came to be tangled up in such a treacherous web will be told in the next chapter.

Chapter 37

The Kidnap of Mary Queen of Scots: Rape, Sexual Violence and Coercion in Tudor Times

Most historians agree that where Mary Queen of Scots is concerned they can't really agree on anything whatsoever. Even what she actually looked like can take up several pages worth of speculation in one of the weightier tomes concerned with her life and times. And as much as her complicity in the murder of her second husband, Lord Darnley, remains a mystery, so also do the circumstances that led from there into her third and final marriage, to the chief suspect in the case, the Earl of Bothwell. A woman of ever-simmering passions, Mary Queen of Scots certainly never did things by halves.

After the murder of her husband, Darnley, and with the nobility of Scotland thrown into a state of disarray, Mary turned to Bothwell because he was unflinchingly loyal to the crown, unlike the majority of the other nobles, most of whom were Protestants, and most of whom would have sold their own mothers into slavery if they thought it might make them a quick shilling. Bothwell was a Protestant too, but for him the queen still came ahead of his religious loyalty, and he had been as unflinchingly devoted to her mother, Mary of Guise, as well. He was also one of the few nobles who wasn't secretly on the payroll of the English and had in fact spent a short time imprisoned in the Tower of London for various offences.

In the wake of Darnley's murder, Bothwell asked Mary to marry him but she refused, and so he petitioned the various Scottish lords to put the proposal to her on his behalf instead, plying them with generous doses of beer, wine, and also a series of thinly veiled threats, all for the express purpose of backing him in making a more formal proposal. Still the queen refused his offer. The scene of this purported exercise in alcoholic bribery was Ainslie's Tavern in Edinburgh, whose exact location has puzzled aficionados of Mary's story for centuries since. Suggested locations have ranged from somewhere on the Royal Mile right down to a small pub ensconced somewhere in the grounds of Holyrood Palace itself. Either way, the ruse worked, and the bond put forth by Bothwell was signed by some eight bishops, nine earl and seven lords. In true tradition of Scottish lords and nobles, they were later to go back on the word of this bond and metaphorically stab Bothwell in the back, but that was still several months away. For now, they were content to see him move to take the throne, and to wonder then whether or not he would provide sufficient force to remove Scotland from the political quagmire in which it currently found itself.

Bothwell's complicity in the murder of Darnley had actually been cleared by an official court – Mary was seen waving to him from a window in Holyrood on the day he was due to be tried – though on subsequent nights placards were being posted up in Edinburgh accusing him of the crime, with the queen as his accomplice. The most infamous of these placards depicted Mary as a mermaid – the symbol at the time of a prostitute – sitting astride Bothwell's Hepburn family crest, the symbol of which was a hare. It has to be said that her behaviour with Bothwell was on the borderline of indiscretion, which points to the fact that she was either besotted with him or in such deep shock at the series of savage events that she didn't really know what she was doing and was simply clinging to anyone offering comfort and security. It is possible that she may also have been suffering from some degree of postnatal depression, the effects of which were barely understood at the time. Either way, such behaviour did little to endear her to her cousin, the queen of England, who continued to admonish her on the example her behaviour was setting. Elizabeth I came from the school of hard knocks and was readily equipped by the travails of her life – including that stint in the Tower of London – to be a queen, whereas Mary's cossetted upbringing in France had clearly left her ill-prepared for the realities of ruling a country and navigating the potential pitfalls involved with all of the warring personalities. However, for those who attempt to paint a picture of these two women as lifelong rivals, it has to be said that at this particular point in Mary's life Elizabeth seemed genuinely concerned for her welfare on a personal level, despite her concerns of the more general tarnishing of the Scottish crown.

On 24 April 1567 Mary and a small entourage were intercepted by Bothwell and a band of his men on the way back from Stirling Castle where she had been visiting her son. She and her followers were then effectively 'kidnapped', although there was no skirmish as such. The royal entourage were vastly outnumbered and Mary made it clear that the few men she had with her were to offer no resistance. A messenger was, however, sent back to Edinburgh and cannons were fired on the party but they were by that time too far away. There is some doubt as to the veracity of this particular portion of the story, however. Such an action could have had the adverse effect of atomising* the queen as well as her captor, and one must therefore treat it with a sensible amount of caution. (*There was a very real risk that the queen and her party might have been blown up by the very same people who were trying to rescue them.)

Mary and her retinue were taken some several miles, eventually arriving at Bothwell's sea fortress of Dunbar Castle, where she had fled after the murder of Rizzio, and where she was now to be 'ravished' by Bothwell and thereby honour-bound to marry him as a result of the trespass on her body. For centuries historians have wrangled with the writers of romantic fiction over whether the whole thing was a set-up, and whether the star-crossed Scots lovers were having a good laugh at the expense of the entire population, or whether or not Mary really was an innocent pawn in the plans of an ambitious and unscrupulous nobleman. The jury is still out in this regard, and the crumbling walls of what remains of Dunbar Castle continue to hold their secrets, as well as their nesting gulls. Academics such as Retha Warnicke are very much of the mind that Mary had been raped by Bothwell: 'Others in her train, like James Melville, who later recalled that Bothwell boasted he would marry his royal captive whether she would or would not have him, would surely have summoned aid if they had not feared the reprisals of this powerful earl who could rally thousands of lieges for support' (Warnicke, 2006, p153). However, it must be noted that much of what Melville recalled was said when he was an old man, and he was certainly no supporter of Bothwell.

John Guy, perhaps Mary's most eminent modern biographer, is, however, very much of the opinion that Mary was in love with Bothwell, that the kidnap culminated in the earl winning Mary over by showing her that he had the support of the Scottish lords whom he had petitioned for backing, and that physical coercion was not necessary. 'Mary was a woman of spirit: high-minded and fully conscious of her "grandeur" as a Queen. It is entirely out of character that she would ever have married Bothwell if he had raped her. It is sometimes claimed that he was the first man who satisfied her sexually. That is perfectly possible, given the Dauphin's ill-health and puny physique and Darnley's sheer selfishness. And yet, even if it is true, it is a world apart from saying that Mary could ever have forgiven Bothwell for forcing her into bed against her will' (Guy, 2009, p329).

Guy's version of events seems to have won out in recent times, with the 2018 blockbuster movie starring Saoirse Ronan as Mary being based fairly firmly on his biography, although the actual pairing of Mary and Bothwell borrows quite substantially from Warnicke's version of events as well. Most of the other cinematic outings for Mary have treated her relationship with Bothwell in a far more romantic light than the sordid reality of Warnicke's version. The 1936 movie *Mary of Scotland* has Katharine Hepburn swooning upon the battlements of Dunbar Castle as she is romanced by Frederic March's purring, sultry Bothwell, while the 1971 film starring Vanessa Redgrave as Mary has her falling for the slightly more earthy charms of Nigel Davenport's Bothwell. Likewise, the 2004 mini-series *Gunpowder, Treason and Plot* graphically portrays the passionate affair that Mary and Bothwell are said to have embarked upon.

Documenting the various different portrayals of the relationship is, if nothing else, a fascinating exercise on marking out how attitudes towards sexual coercion have changed over the years. There was at the time that Mary was taken to Dunbar Castle a caveat in the law whereby a woman might be forced to marry her assailant because she was considered 'damaged goods', or because it was perceived that she was required to restore 'her honour' in this manner after the attack. How this particular piece of patriarchy played into events is open to interpretation, but Mary may have realised soon afterwards that she was pregnant by Bothwell, and may thus have consented to marriage in order to avoid the taint of illegitimacy being foisted upon her unborn child or children.

Mary eventually returned to the capital, with Bothwell holding the bridle of her horse to signify that he now had 'custody' of her person. Less than a month later they were officially married at Holyrood Palace in a Protestant ceremony that apparently so traumatised Mary, in regard to the betrayal of her Catholic faith, that she became in subsequent days extremely distraught, even to the point of wishing herself actual physical harm. Little more than a month later Bothwell had fled from the field of battle and Mary herself was a prisoner of her rebellious, backstabbing lords and nobles, soon to be locked up in the little island castle of Lochleven...

Chapter 38

The Calamity on Carberry Hill

Before Mary Queen of Scots ended up being imprisoned in Lochleven Castle, she still had to be separated from her new husband, the Earl of Bothwell, and that meant a confrontation with her backstabbing Protestant lords and nobles. This 'battle' – one of the single biggest 'non-events' in all of Scottish history – occurred on Carberry Hill near Musselburgh, just outside of Edinburgh, where a plaque mounted by the Marie Stuart Society now marks the rough spot of the non-confrontation.

After Mary and Bothwell's forces were lured from the relative safety of Dunbar Castle and onto the aforementioned site, the two sides soon found themselves caught up in a classic Mexican standoff. Mary and Bothwell's men atop a hill and baking in the scorching June sun, while the opposing army fared slightly better from a vantage point further down the field and near to the replenishing waters of a river. In the end, after Bothwell had challenged various of the cowardly lords to man-to-man combat – all offers were either refused or seriously stalled – Mary managed to negotiate a safe escape for him and then trustingly handed herself over to the opposing side.

She had never been a particularly good judge of character, but this particular lack of judgement has to stand head and shoulders above all of her other dire decisions, bar the one that led her to embark on a journey to England seeking Elizabeth Tudor's help. While Bothwell rode off to relative safety, the opposing army promptly surrounded their 'beloved' queen and proceeded to hurl all sorts of vitriol in her direction, before hauling her off on a scenic tour of Edinburgh, including an impromptu procession past the site of Kirk O'Field, where her second husband had been murdered. After this, they locked her up in a house near the current Royal Mile. The house was referred to back then as the 'Black Turnpike'. Mary was by that time exhausted and dishevelled, hungry, and dressed still in the dusty clothes that she had been kitted out with back at Dunbar

Castle: 'Those of a tradesman's wife. So she put on the red petticoat and a black velvet hat, a scarf was found for her, and the sleeves of her bodice were tied with points' (Plaidy, 1978, p144).

Foolishly imagining that the citizens of Scotland didn't regard her as a scarlet woman who had murdered her effeminate husband in order to marry her swaggering, rough lover, Mary then threw open the windows to the little room in which she'd been imprisoned and begged the crowds outside for their help in freeing her from her despicable bondage. They responded by waving a banner under which her rebellious lords had marched at Carberry Hill. It had a picture of her infant son, James, observing his father's corpse, alongside the words 'Judge and revenge my cause, O Lord', taken to some extent from the drawing made of the murder scene at Kirk O'Field. Besides that, they also hurled more abuse and vitriol, and according to some accounts also some pieces of rotten fruit. Needless to say, Mary had to be moved away from the window for her own safety.

A short while later she tried again to enlist the help of the crowd, this time becoming so frantic that she apparently tore at her clothes and hair and ended up almost hanging topless out of the window before the guards inside the Black Turnpike restrained her once more. At this point some of the crowd were moved to pity by the sight of their queen in such a calamitous state, although not so very moved that they actually made any serious attempt to try and free her. The next day, Mary was marched back down the Royal Mile and into Holyrood Palace under strict armed guard, at which point her spirits must surely have rallied. She was safely back in the royal residence, even if Bothwell was miles away and doing who knows what (he was in fact trying to raise support for a fightback, although in the end he was pursued and forced to flee the country). Back at Holyrood Palace, Mary was given a brief meal and a reunion with her ladies-in-waiting before being told that she was soon to be going on a little journey.

As for Bothwell, well, he tried his best to rally support for Mary, but was chased out of Scotland by the emergent new regime. Various sea battles ensued, before bad weather drove him and his ships to Norway. From there, Bothwell was escorted to the port of Bergen, where he had the immense misfortune to run into a disgruntled ex-wife. She now wielded considerable influence and was able to have him imprisoned in Bergenhus fortress, whereby she was able to attempt to reclaim some of her dowry and also to sue him for abandonment. King Frederick of Denmark, meanwhile, had gotten wind of the fact that Bothwell was, according to the new regime in Scotland, wanted in connection with the murder of Darnley. On that basis, Frederick decided to keep hold of Bothwell, perhaps with the intention of ransoming him off to the highest bidder. The English were also said to have been very interested in bringing him to justice. Bothwell was then imprisoned in Malmo Castle, before word reached Frederick that Mary was unlikely ever to become Queen of Scots again. Her dramatic fall from power was by this time well underway. Bothwell, at least as a bargaining chip, was therefore redundant.

From Malmo Castle Bothwell was then transported to Dragsholm Castle, where he spent the last few years of his life in a dungeon, chained to a pillar and slowly losing both his mind and his dignity. The pillar is still extant and retains the circular groove in the floor all around it, worn down due to his constant, wearied pacing. When he finally died in 1578 it was undoubtedly a mercy, for he was by that time insane and literally caked in his own filth. He was buried at a church near to the castle, where his body was on display for various periods (urban legend has it that the head was used as a football by the local children). Scotland has never laid claim to the body, as is the case of the still-missing corpse of James IV. A husk said to be Bothwell's body was displayed in the Edinburgh Wax Museum from 1976, although the provenance of the remains has never been satisfactorily explained. Pictures of the mummified head can be found quite easily online and in displays in the Mary Queen of Scots' visitor centre in Jedburgh.

It was at Jedburgh that Mary fell ill after making her dash to see a wounded Bothwell at his stronghold of Hermitage Castle. She was so ill that it was feared that she would never recover, collapsing after a severe pain in her left side and then vomiting large quantities of blood. For the next few days she drifted in and out of consciousness in the building that now serves as the aforementioned visitor centre, suffering also from convulsions, losing the power of speech, and, on one occasion, also her sight. At one point her limbs quite suddenly stiffened, and her body temperature cooled to the point where it appeared that she had lost the battle for life. The quick action of her surgeon, Charles Nau, saved her. He bandaged her limbs to the point of rigidity and also administered some sort of an enema, as well as forcing her mouth open and frequently pouring into it small amounts of wine. The enema set off a chain of vomiting and diarrhoea, accompanied by quantities of 'old' blood.

Her recovery followed on soon after, although the precise nature of the attack – Mary was to suffer several such incidents during the course of her life – has for the most part eluded historical confirmation. The most common diagnosis delivered is that of porphyria. This is a disorder of the liver that can display multiple symptoms, including the abdominal pain that Mary suffered, along with the vomiting and also the paralysis and seizures. However, several historians have speculated that on this occasion she may have been laid low by the bursting of a gastric ulcer. The said ulcer would have been reared on a steady diet of Darnley-related stress, as well as her fearing for the life of Bothwell, whom she may already have begun to see as some sort of a saviour against the onslaught of her various woes. It is of course worth noting that any retrospective diagnosis is fraught with inconsistencies and therefore can only be spurious at best.

Chapter 39

Lochleven: Political Imprisonment

After her separation from Bothwell and her subsequent capture by her rebellious lord and nobles, the destination of Mary Queen of Scots' journey from Holyrood Palace was revealed to be the island castle of Lochleven, near Kinross, a small, sturdy stronghold only accessible by boat. On her way there the disgraced queen frequently slowed her horse in the hope that she might be shortly rescued by those of her supporters who still remained at liberty, but no help was forthcoming. On her arrival on the island, after being rowed across the loch, Mary promptly took to her bed for a fortnight, refusing to either speak or eat. Her situation eventually became so dire that her captors feared that she would not survive, that her recent trials had indeed broken her seemingly indomitable spirit, though there seems to be no indication that she suffered from the kind of physical collapse that had befallen her at Jedburgh.

Not long after, when she was at least up and taking food, Mary nearly *did* die when she miscarried Bothwell's child; or children, as it has been stated by various sources that she was in fact carrying twins. Further legend has it that the child, or one at least *one* of the children, was then smuggled off the island and taken to France, where she grew up to be a nun. For those pernickety historians particularly bothered by their blood pressure in relation to such unfounded rumours, it needs be said here that they may want to seek an alternative to the rather large dose of salt that should accompany the swallowing of this particular tale.

In a roughly related aside, it is worth mentioning that Mary's son, James, was said to have perished shortly after his birth in Edinburgh Castle, back in 1566, and that another child was hurriedly substituted in his place. This rumour was further lent credence when a small coffin was found which contained the skeleton of an infant child, walled up inside the castle during renovations in 1830 following a fire. It was widely believed that the unfortunate child may have been simply the sadly deceased offspring of a serving maid, although for conspiracy theorists this was grist to the mill; such a tale was too well-spun to be true. When James was born, rumours had already begun to circulate that he was in fact the son of David Rizzio, so questions in regard to his paternity/ claim to the throne were nothing new, even if they took on rather a more macabre aspect in the instance of the discovery of the dead baby. Furthermore, James apparently looked nothing like his more attractive parents, although it isn't unknown for genes to skip a generation or two, but this merely serves to prove the point for those who believe that there had in fact been a substitution due to some sort of mishap.

After the miscarriage in Lochleven, regardless of how many children she actually lost, Mary was left in an extremely vulnerable position. It was in this weakened state that the rebellious lords put to her the proposition that she should abdicate her throne at once, and that her baby son, James, should be crowned instead. With a monarch at such a tender age Scotland would of course need a regent, and Mary's duplicitous half-brother, Moray, was more than willing to step into the breach until the boy came of age.

Weakened and wearied as she was, Mary still refused to sign the deed of abdication, at which point she was threatened with being cut up into 'collops' (a slice of meat) if she did not put her signature to the abdication paper (the various slices of dismembered Scots queen would then be cast into the lake around the island for the fish to feed upon). Mary had suffered similar such threats in the immediate aftermath of the murder of David Rizzio, but by now she was utterly drained after her defeat at Carberry Hill, from losing Bothwell and then losing her children too. In the face of such blatant intimidation, Mary had little choice but to sign her name to the abdication deed, although she did so under considerable protest and was later to deem the action effectively null and void due to the level of coercion employed. Not long afterwards, Sir William Douglas, Mary's custodian while she was in Lochleven 'sang lustily in his garden and danced a jog, though he refused at first to tell his captive what he was celebrating so wildly. When he asked laughingly why she, too, was not celebrating her son's coronation Mary wept aloud, calling on God to avenge her' (Mackay, 2000, p222).

All in all, Mary Queen of Scots spent almost a year trapped in the castle on the little island on Loch Leven, living in relative comfort but also in some considerable boredom, writing letters to anyone who might help her, even by using the soot from the chimney for ink when her captors denied her those most basic of amenities. At this point in her predicament her cousin Elizabeth was still on her side, sending various envoys up to Scotland to see if they could either secure Mary's release or at least better treatment for her.

Shrewd as she was, Elizabeth may have been watching the proceedings in Scotland and wondering whether or not such a similar fate might one day befall her. She was a woman ruler as well, and, unlike Mary, had been ruling without benefit of any male counsel, however much her court may have wished otherwise. Therefore, it wasn't a great stretch of the imagination for Elizabeth to consider that her own subjects might follow the Scottish example and swiftly lock her up in the Tower of London on some flimsy patriarchal pretext, which meant that it was in her interest to see the rightful order of things restored as soon as possible, as much as Mary's behaviour may have galled her in various other respects.

The idea of a destabilised and powerless Mary may also have had something of a wider appeal, to her ministers if not to Elizabeth personally. After the merciless debacle of Mary Tudor ('Bloody Mary'), no Catholic was ever likely to be allowed to so much as even sneeze in the direction of the English throne. It is perhaps worth noting that at this time Elizabeth was actually engaged in a bidding war with Catherine de Medici over several of Mary's more luxurious jewels, ransacked and then confiscated from the fallen queen's various properties by her treacherous half-brother, so exactly how much solidarity there still was in the royal 'sisterhood' is perhaps somewhat still open to question. Appearances may have mattered to Elizabeth I, but none more so than her own personal reflection.

Mary's tragic charm led several of Lochleven's young male residents to fall for her: 'pretty' George Douglas and 'Little' Willie Douglas, to be precise. Between the two of them they began to hatch plans to prise the queen from captivity and spirit her away to the mainland, where support for Mary – not to mention opposition to Moray's rule – was already growing fast. George Douglas was Moray's half-brother, and also brother to Sir William Douglas, while 'Little' Willie was an orphan of dubious origin and may have been an illegitimate child of Sir William. The bastard offspring of nobles and their unfortunate servants peppered the landscapes around the royal residences of Scotland and England with almost as much abundance as did the various flora and fauna.

Given his pedigree, George was seen as a potential suitor for Mary and therefore Sir William's wife, Margaret Erskine – Moray's mother and therefore also former mistress of Mary's father, James V – was torn between being a harsh jailer and also trying to keep sweet the woman who might one day become her daughter-in-law. She also had to contend with the fact that her prisoner was still of the blood royal herself, even if she was no longer a reigning queen. As far as Mary's second saviour was concerned, 'little Willie' was by all accounts something of a handful, frequently flaunting the gold coins given to him by the queen in return for ferrying back and forth valuable snippets of information to the outside world. Both he and George were to find themselves expelled from the island at various points because of their plotting in order to free Mary, but both would eventually find that family affection allowed them back into the fold and thus allow for further plotting. Had they not managed to inveigle their way back onto the island then it is quite possible that Mary may have spent the rest of her days there. Considering what was to come, one can only wonder whether that was perhaps something of a blessing.

One early attempt at escape from Lochleven Castle saw Mary disguising herself as one of the laundresses who travelled to the island to do the washing for the residents. She actually got as far as boarding the small boat heading away from the island before she was discovered. For a few short moments it must have seemed that her bid for freedom had been successful, when quite suddenly one of the men rowing tried to snatch her muffler from her face. Quite why he did this remains unclear, but he may simply have been making a pass at this new and rather coy laundress. When Mary tried to resist, mainly by pulling the muffler back into place, her lily-white hands gave her away. She was promptly rowed back to the island but the men kept quiet about the escape attempt; there were loyalists to the queen all over, it seems. There were also abortive plans to spirit her away when she was taken hawking on one of the other islands on Loch Leven, but these were dismissed for a variety of reasons as being too risky. It wasn't that long after these various abortive attempts that George Douglas was dismissed from the island for what appeared to have been the final time. By then, he seemed to have secured a plan of action by taking with him one of Mary's earrings as a sign of fealty. It had been arranged with the queen that when the earring was returned to her then another escape attempt was imminent. In the event, it turned out that she didn't have long to wait.

Mary's next bid for freedom from Lochleven was far more successful. On 2 May 1568 the deposed queen managed to pull off one of the most spectacular romantic escapes in history. Vast quantities of wine, alongside ladies-in-waiting deployed as decoys and sabotaged boats all had their part to play in the unfolding drama, culminating with Mary brazenly walking out of the castle gates in full view of her captors, albeit in disguise. It was an escape in scale and also in sheer farce to match anything seen on *Prisoner Cell Block H*. For starters, 'Little' Willie Douglas had tampered with all of the boats tethered to the island except for the one to be used for the escape, before then snatching the keys from under the eyes of Sir William Douglas by throwing his handkerchief over them as he capered around the dinner table in his guise as 'the lord of misrule'. By this time those vast quantitates of wine were making their presence felt, possibly having been drugged, to boot. Earlier, Willie had been spotted in that self-same act of 'pegging' the boats by Sir William, who was then deftly distracted by Mary as she pretended suddenly to feel faint. Then, as Margaret Erskine and Mary were strolling on the island shore they spotted a group of horsemen gathering on the mainland. Margaret Erskine was all for sounding the alarm, but Mary, assuming they might be scouts for her forthcoming rescuers, deployed a distraction by unleashing a verbal diatribe against Margaret's favourite son, her own half-brother, Moray. Again, it worked, and the escape attempt went ahead as planned.

As Willie Douglas rowed Mary to safety across the loch, he tossed the keys to the castle gates into the water, from where they were eventually recovered several hundred years later when the loch was partially drained. A different take on the tale has Willie tossing the keys into the mouth of a nearby cannon, which kills the authenticity of the whole 'tossed into the loch' line, unless the cannon happened to be one of those used to fire at the escaping boat, in which case it all ties together rather nicely. The purported keys have passed through various exhibitions regarding Mary's life over the last several decades and are currently in the possession of the National Museums of Scotland.

Mary's lady-in-waiting, Mary Seton, had been employed as a decoy, apparently dressing as the queen and standing rather visibly in one of the castle windows while her mistress was busily being spirited away. Despite her part in the escape plot, Mary Seton was soon freed from Lochleven and was then able to rejoin her mistress when eventually she ended up in England. The various ruses and diversions had worked and Mary Queen of Scots was once more a free woman. Quite how long she would be able to retain her freedom was another matter entirely.

After her escape from Lochleven, Mary enjoyed a few fleeting weeks of freedom before circumstances forced her to face down her half-brother's forces at the small village of Langside, not far from Glasgow. A bond was drawn up beforehand, stating that Mary's abdication had been given under duress – the threat of 'collops' was perhaps quoted in this regard – that Moray's rule was treasonable, and that the queen was to be restored to her throne forthwith. Despite the fact that almost any bond signed by a Scottish noble wasn't worth the paper it was written on, Mary's hopes must have been soaring. Her intended destination was Dumbarton Castle, from where she had sailed to France some years previously, and from where she would comfortably be able to sit and wait for reinforcements from the north to arrive. Mary observed the battle at Langside on a mound near Cathcart Castle. A monument now rather morbidly marks the spot where her hopes for restoration were rather rudely dashed. After a mere forty-five minutes or so, Mary's men were thoroughly defeated. Mary apparently lost her legendary bottle and promptly fled the scene, crossing down through Scotland over several days and nights in a desperate dash to avoid recapture. There are several further monuments to this battle in Langside for the Marian enthusiast to visit when passing through the city, alongside the one mentioned near Cathcart Castle.

Back at Loch Leven, poor Sir William Douglas had meanwhile tried to stab himself, so great was his shame at having failed to prevent the escape of his royal captive. He survived the attempt, indicating that his heart perhaps wasn't quite in it. Meanwhile, Mary and her small party of loyal lords made for the safety of Dundrennan Abbey in present-day Dumfries and Galloway, moving only at night in order to avoid being spotted. More legends percolate around this desperate escape, including the story that Mary was given food and shelter – a bowl of sour milk, by all accounts – in what was effectively a peasant's cottage, the occupant being rewarded for their hospitality with the gift of the land on which the property stood. Mary was to write the following words to one of her French uncles; 'I have endured injuries, calumnies, imprisonment, famine, cold, hear, flight not knowing whither, 92 miles across the country without stopping or alighting, and then I have had to sleep upon the ground and drink sour milk, and eat oatmeal without bread, and have been for three nights likes the owls.'

Once at Dundrennan Abbey, Mary made perhaps *the* most ill-informed of all her various dire missteps, a misjudgement of character concerning her cousin Queen Elizabeth I so very colossal that it seems to the modern historian almost an act of sheer madness. Despite the pleadings of the lords and nobles who had fled with her, and who wanted her to go to France and seek refuge there instead, Mary had decided to fling herself on the mercy of her older Protestant cousin. Given that Mary's former mother-in-law was Catherine de Medici and given that Catherine was very much alive and in power in the French court, it is to some extent possible to understand Mary's reasoning. Simply put, the relatively unknown quantity of Elizabeth Tudor may have been more preferable than a return to the scorn and scrutiny of a woman Mary had once apparently had the misfortune to mistake for a commoner. On that basis, she and said nobles boarded a small fishing boat and made the perilous crossing over the Solway Firth to the little port of Workington in England. A monument (yes, another one) has since been erected near the spot (on the English side), marking the point at which the beginnings of Mary's monumental woes as a political prisoner really began.

She was never to set foot in Scotland again.

Chapter 40

It's Grim Up North:
The 1569 Northern Rebellion

The arrival of Mary Queen of Scots in England after her escape from Lochleven and her subsequent defeat in Glasgow was a source of embarrassment, dilemma and above all danger for Elizabeth I and for England as a whole. Mary arrived on English soil already well on her way to becoming the romantic, tragic heroine of myth. She was also almost ten years younger than Elizabeth, and a famed beauty with at least one purported stalker under her belt, whereas Elizabeth relied more on rhetoric than the Tudor equivalent of Revlon to get her point across. Perhaps most pertinent of all, Mary was of course also a Catholic and considered by many Catholics in England – not to mention most of Europe – to be the rightful heir to the throne of England after 'Bloody' Mary Tudor, with Elizabeth herself cast as the usurping bastard begotten by that infamous courtesan, Anne Boleyn. It probably would have been far better for everyone concerned if Mary had gone to France instead, but, as previously stated, when your former mother-in-law was Catherine de Medici, it's easy to see why she might have baulked at the suggestion and plumped for her vain, suspicious 'sister queen' instead.

At first, Mary and her small entourage were treated well enough, with Mary herself fêted as though she were a royal 'guest', but in fact she was already little more than a prisoner. She enjoyed one night of relative freedom at Workington Hall (which is now a ruined shell) before Elizabeth's guards arrived to 'escort' her to a more secure environment. Mary thus spent a short stint in Carlisle Castle, confined for the most part in a now-demolished part of the building, but accompanied by her ever-expanding entourage, including many who followed her from Scotland several weeks after the debacle outside Glasgow. These adherents included Mary Seton, of the famous Four Marys, liberated from Lochleven and now on hand to coiffure Mary's hair every morning so that she might face her jailers in the latest fashion, if nothing else. Wigs of various colours and designs were also involved, by all accounts, which has led – some several hundred years later – to endless agonised debate as to what Mary's natural hair colour actually was. During her time at Carlisle Castle, Mary was allowed to attend church services and was also said to have observed what may have been one of the first ever recorded football matches, but behind the scenes things were moving at a far more rapid pace than an impromptu five-a-side, and not at all in her favour.

Eventually, Mary and her entourage were moved further south to Bolton Castle in Yorkshire, a great deal further away from the Scottish border, thus making any attempt at a rescue all the more arduous. It was while at Bolton Castle, and after a show trial to consider her complicity in the murder of Darnley, that it was decided to keep Mary more permanently as a 'guest'/state prisoner of England. This show trial involved the production in 'court' of the infamous 'casket letters', a selection of poems, missives and other dubiously incriminating documents said to have been written from Mary to Bothwell, the whole sorry lot purporting to offer some sort of evidence that she and he had conspired to kill Darnley and rule Scotland from the very start.

Yet again, historical opinion on the veracity of the casket letters remains divided, but the majority opinion seems to indicate that they are rather ham-fisted fakes, whereby phrases from some of Mary's genuine letters were extrapolated and reimagined into some sort of tawdry conspiracy, laced with a bit of adultery for good measure. Even more astonishing than the lack of quality in producing these counterfeits is the fact that people swallowed them hook, line and sinker. Then again, there were a great many people who had a lot to profit if Mary were to be kept out of circulation permanently. The fact that they were produced as evidence by Mary's treacherous half-brother, Moray, gives an idea of just how dubiously one ought to view them.

From Bolton Castle Mary was entrusted into the care/custody of the 6th Earl of Shrewsbury, George Talbot, and his wife, the notorious Tudor battle-axe, Bess of Hardwick. Mary made the move from the relative comfort of Bolton Castle to her new 'residence' of Tutbury Castle in Staffordshire in shocking January winter weather, stopping at several points along the way because the roads were impassable or because one or another of her entourage had fallen ill as a result of the appalling weather. Tutbury Castle was a place that Mary would come to liken –

over the course of several lengthy sojourns – as being almost akin to an open-air toilet, with facilities so inadequate even on this initial stay that local grand houses in the immediate vicinity had to be ransacked for their goods, the better to make her comfortable, alongside having furnishings sent all the way up from the Tower of London. The Earl of Shrewsbury was possessed of so many castles and grand manor houses that he can be forgiven for letting one or two of them to fall into neglect, although Tutbury remained an unappealing prospect even when decked out with all the finery that other local establishments had to offer. As for the Shrewsburys, they seem at first to have been quite dazzled by the fact of being appointed custodians to a fallen, romantic queen. It would be several years, and several treacherous plots later that they would begin to realise what a poisoned chalice they had been handed.

It was during one of Mary's initial stays at Tutbury that the north of England began to rumble with the first overtures of rebellion, with Mary as the focal point for the disaffected Catholic gentry. How much she knew of this rising or even encouraged it is, as always, open to debate, but it is possible that Mary may in fact have discouraged the movement as being harmful both to her cause and also to the cause of the Catholics in England. At this point she can have had scant idea that she would be spending the next several decades there, after all. However, as far as the realm of fiction is concerned, she was actually egging the rebels on for all she was worth, as typified in Philippa Gregory's novel *The Other Queen*: 'I am trembling with excitement and I cannot hide it. I cannot make my face serene or my voice calm. I am a French princess, I should be under complete self-control, but I want to dance around the room and scream, with delight. It seems that the storm I have summoned has broken on England like a great wave at sea. My army has won the whole of the North, and today captured the port of Hartlepool for the Spanish armada, which will land there. The Pope will declare for me, and order every Roman Catholic in England to take arms for me' (Gregory, 2011, p222).

The novel – and many other sources besides – also say that Shrewsbury was at this point quite madly in love with Mary. He wasn't so smitten that he ever actually helped her to try and escape, but it isn't impossible that his infatuation may have been better served by having her exactly where he could see her. While Mary's confinement was fairly rigorous, it should be noted that at this point she still had a fairly large entourage and was waited on in the manner befitting a queen, albeit a deposed one. She was served countless courses for all of her meals and still sat under a cloth of state, in a kind of 'mock court', the semblance of which must have helped greatly in keeping her from a total mental collapse. At this stage she was also on fairly friendly terms with Bess of Hardwick, the two of them whiling away the hours sewing and gossiping. The verbal material from these embroidery sessions would later help shape a scandalous letter that Mary was to send to Elizabeth when she and Bess had fallen out, and when Mary was thus seeking to preserve what little remained of her tattered reputation. Apparently, Elizabeth Tudor never saw the contents of this highly embarrassing document, but had she done so it was quite possible that she would have had Bess of Hardwick executed on the spot, old friends or no. According to Mary's letter, Bess and various other ladies-in-waiting had quite literally laughed behind Elizabeth's back at the scale of her monstrous vanity – and that was just the tip of the scandalous iceberg that Mary had unleashed. But all of this was well over a decade into the future.

By November 1569 all of the pieces of the prospective rebellion were well in place, and on 9 November the rising began, with the Earls of Westmorland and Northumberland and their respective armies marching south under a banner depicting the Five Wounds of Christ. This was the designated symbol of the new rebellion, akin to that used during the Pilgrimage of Grace in the reign of Henry VIII. Their mission was to restore Catholicism and perhaps place Mary Queen of Scots on the throne. Some historians have cited the presence of the Scots queen in England so soon before the rising, and therefore a potential rallying factor, as nothing more than a coincidence. Either way, in a mad dash to keep her out of their hands, Elizabeth I ordered Shrewsbury to move Mary farther south – to Coventry, in fact – where she spent the next several months, ferried from one nobleman's house to another, waiting on tenterhooks to see how things would pan out.

This was probably the closest that Mary ever got to becoming queen of England, with Elizabeth herself retreating to the security of Windsor Castle in order to sit things out. When the promised Spanish aid for the rebellion failed to materialise, the uprising rapidly petered out and the normal folk returned home with their pitchforks between their legs, just in time for Christmas and a series of savage Elizabethan reprisals that would have made her father truly proud. The Earl of Westmorland managed to make it safely to the Continent, where he died penniless and all but forgotten by everyone. By contrast, the Earl of Northumberland fled to Scotland, where he was captured and then ransomed back to the English for a hefty sum. He was beheaded in York on 22 August 1572 and was then beatified by the Pope in 1895 for his services to the Catholic Church. It was mooted at this point that Mary might be removed from the Shrewsbury household and given over to a far less considerate custodian, but in the end she remained with them for almost another fifteen years, resulting in the painfully slow disintegration of their marriage and almost a state of penury for the good earl himself.

Chapter 41

The Ridolfi Plot: Tudor Intrigues

You can't keep a good queen down and Mary Queen of Scots didn't let the defeat of the 1569 rebellion dishearten her too much. As she began the first of a series of lengthy sojourns in Sheffield Castle (another Shrewsbury property), she also began corresponding, for a second time, with her prospective fourth husband, the Duke of Norfolk, who just happened to be one of Elizabeth's premier noblemen. The duke had been mooted as a husband for Mary as far back as her show trial at Bolton Castle, and had then been pinpointed as a potential king of England in the event that the 1569 rebellion succeeded. Now, despite his better judgement, he decided to throw in his lot with the captive queen for a second time, only now he was enlisting the help of the Florentine banker Roberto Ridolfi in a bid to incite an invasion against England.

Like many of the plots orchestrated by – or at least *purported* to have been orchestrated by – Mary Queen of Scots against Elizabeth I during the former's confinement in England, the ins and outs, or the 'who did what and who said what to whom' of the Ridolfi Plot are so confused and convoluted that even after a span of some four hundred-odd years it is difficult to discern the truth from the tittle-tattle. The basic gist of it seems to be that one of Mary's most loyal supporters, the Bishop of Ross, was used as a go-between to ferry letters back and forth between the various plotters, as the idea of a Spanish invasion to overthrow Elizabeth and place Mary and Norfolk on the thrones of England and Scotland began to take shape.

Mary was at this point shuttling forth between Tutbury Castle, Wingfield Manor and the aforementioned Sheffield Castle, where she actually spent the majority of her time in English captivity. This imposing fortress was razed to the ground after being held by the Royalists during the English Civil War, but recent excavations have discovered that a great deal of the foundations remain relatively intact. The letters conveyed by the Bishop of Ross were smuggled out of Sheffield Castle in a variety of inventive ways, including being inserted into hollow shoe heels, as well as being woven into some of the more elaborate hair arrangements of Mary's female staff. At this point, without any concrete evidence of her plotting, security around Mary was still rather on the lax side. On receipt of these various missives, Roberto Ridolfi travelled Europe to canvass support for the venture, even securing an audience with Pope Pius V, who promised both spiritual and financial backing for the scheme. Pius had previously 'described Elizabeth as a heretic and invited Catholics to depose her, almost the equivalent of an Islamic *fatwa*' (Lovell, 2006, p229). And then, as was apt to happen with so many of Mary's plots, it rather abruptly went pear-shaped.

Charles Baillie, an agent of Roberto Ridolfi, was arrested at the port in Dover in April 1571, and found to be carrying incriminating letters concerning the queen of Scots and her confederates, although they were at that point still in rather a complex cipher. Baillie was then taken to the Marshalsea prison in Southwark, later to be the residence of the father of Charles Dickens, until he cleared his debts. Under torture, Baillie rapidly revealed the various codes for the ciphers, and other arrests soon followed. The Duke of Norfolk's correspondence miscarried itself into the hands of Sir William Cecil, and other letters from Mary to Norfolk were soon found in his London residence, hidden in a variety of ingenious places. The Bishop of Ross was taken to the Tower of London and had only to be shown a brief glimpse of the rack in order for him to implicate his mistress, accusing her, for starters, of having a hand in the deaths of all her previous husbands.

The Duke of Norfolk was also imprisoned in the Tower, but Elizabeth would end up delaying his death for many months before finally having him executed on Tower Hill on 2 June the following year. It was the first major execution of her reign. Roberto Ridolfi, slippery as an eel, managed to escape, and was eventually made a Florentine senator in 1600. Meanwhile, poor Mary found her household at Sheffield Castle severely cut back as a result of the security breach, and tighter restrictions were imposed on her movements, and on the movements of what remained of the beleaguered household. For days, if not weeks, on end they were confined to their rooms without recourse to fresh air and sunshine, and all of their correspondence was strictly vetted. It was at this point that Mary is said to have lost the services of 'Little' Willie Douglas from Lochleven, after he and several other members of her household were sent forth from Sheffield Castle, never to return.

As with everything pertaining to these plots – and of course to Mary herself – it has been mooted, particularly by Francis Edwards in his book *The Dangerous Queen* – that the Ridolfi Plot was in fact an elaborate sting organised by Sir William Cecil with the express purpose of setting Mary Queen of Scots up for a fall. The point of this, so the theory goes, was so that she would end up being so badly implicated in a supposed plot to have Elizabeth assassinated that the queen would have no choice but to order her execution.

Most certainly this is what actually ended up happening to Mary, but it would take another fifteen years or so before such a sting would bear fruit. Elizabeth was loath to wield the axe against a fellow anointed monarch, after all. But it may also equally be the case – and here many Marian enthusiasts will find themselves flinching at the suggestion – that Mary and Norfolk were indeed guilty as charged in regard to the entirety of the Ridolfi Plot. It is true that in the days following the discovery of the Ridolfi Plot, the English Parliament was baying for the head of the Scottish queen, but in this instance Elizabeth actually stepped in to save her cousin's life. However, with any visible demonstration of Elizabeth's supposed 'concern' there was often a caveat. Rather than executing Mary herself, she tried to have her cousin sent back to Scotland so that they could finish her off instead, and thus be done with it. Elizabeth seems to have been quite happy for Mary to lose her head as long as she herself didn't have to be the one to take the blame for it. In the end, as history has proven, Elizabeth would of course have to face up to that rather unpalatable task in the end.

Chapter 42

The Babington Plot:
Tudor Honeytraps

By the time of the Babington Plot, which was to be Mary Queen of Scots' final conspiracy against Elizabeth I, Mary had been a 'guest' of England for around eighteen years or so. Long gone were the lax days of the Earl of Shrewsbury and his wife, Bess of Hardwick, to be replaced instead by the nit-picking Puritan Sir Amyas Paulet, who treated Mary not as a deposed sovereign but as a troublesome prisoner of state, someone to be belittled and reprimanded at almost every turn. There was no love lost between Mary and her newest jailer, aided by the fact that Paulet was a strict Puritan, someone who viewed the Catholic religion of the deposed queen with considerable, and vocal, scorn.

Before the Babington Plot unfolded, a series of smaller conspiracies – the Throckmorton and Parry Plots respectively – had resulted in Mary being moved from Shrewsbury's custody, with matters not being helped by the fact that Bess of Hardwick had become convinced that her husband harboured a secret desire for the queen of Scots. To this end, Bess even went so far as to spread the preposterous rumour that Mary had borne Shrewsbury several illegitimate children while she was a captive. Things became so bad for the earl and his wife that Elizabeth I was forced at one point to attempt a reconciliation between them, but to no avail. Paulet was therefore considered to be a far more suitable jailer, given that candid loathing for all things Catholic. Mary's famous 'sugared words' would dissolve upon a decidedly sour palate in this regard. It was under Paulet's watchful gaze that the sting of the Babington Plot was allowed to unfold, a honey trap that would see Mary finally facing the scaffold in the great hall at Fotheringay Castle in February 1587. The Earl of Shrewsbury and his wife, meanwhile, went their separate ways, he into the hands of a nubile young mistress and she off to oversee the building of the architectural magnificence that is Hardwick Hall.

The Throckmorton Plot was similar in nature to the Ridolfi Plot, with the main aim being to pluck Mary from obscurity and place her securely on the throne of England, while Elizabeth Tudor was quietly – or not so quietly – done away with. The key conspirator was Sir Francis Throckmorton, who had connections to several members of Elizabeth's household and also her council. This time around, a Spanish invasion of England led by the Duke of Guise would topple the House of Tudor and Roman Catholicism would swiftly be restored in the country.

While in Paris, Sir Francis had met and then conspired with several Catholic exiles who would, when the Throckmorton Plot crumbled, go on to play small but pivotal parts in the Babington Plot. Eventually, Sir Francis returned to England, unaware of the fact that almost his every move was being observed by English spymasters intent on ridding their queen of the scourge of Mary Queen of Scots once and for all. He began carrying letters between Mary, her Parisian plotters and Bernardino de Mendoza, Phillip II's ambassador to the English court. Some of the correspondence was picked up as it passed through the French embassy, and Sir Francis was arrested and taken to the Tower of London, at which point a list of Catholic supporters for the cause was also discovered. For his part in the Throckmorton Plot, de Mendoza was summarily expelled from the country. As for Sir Francis, he was tortured at the Tower, with the intent of discovering every last detail of the conspiracy. He was then executed in July 1584.

The most damning outcome, for Mary at least, was the creation of the Bond of Association, masterminded by Cecil and also by Sir Francis Walsingham. The basic gist of this piece of extremely dubious legislation was the fact that it urged all signatories to execute anyone who made an attempt on the life of Elizabeth I, including those who might somehow benefit from the successful completion of said assassination. This caveat, it was hoped, would allow for the execution of Mary Queen of Scots even if she herself were unaware of the fact that a random bunch of supporters were somewhere plotting to free her. In an attempt to prove her innocence, Mary herself became one of the first signatories of the bond, although it failed in the end to save her from the headsman's axe. By this time, having been in captivity for so very long, Mary would undoubtedly have signed almost anything that might further improve her conditions.

The Parry Plot took place in 1585. It was rather smaller in scale than the vast Eurocentric intricacy of the Ridolfi Plot. Smaller even than the Throckmorton Plot, with its ties to France and Spain. It involved an English courtier called William Parry, who, at some point in his career, then became a Catholic double agent at the centre of a plot to assassinate Elizabeth I. Amidst his see-sawing loyalties, the basic gist of the scheme seems to have been that Parry – perhaps with another gentleman in tow – would shoot Elizabeth while she was out in her carriage, or else murder her during the course of a private audience, probably with a dagger. Whether or not the assassination attempt was ever attempted, Parry was eventually denounced by one of his co-conspirators and taken to the Tower of London, from where he protested his innocence to anyone willing to listen. He was put on trial and pleaded guilty in the hope of gaining some clemency from the court, before abruptly declaring his confession to be false. Either way, the outcome was in little doubt and he was executed on 2 March 1585, on Westminster/Old Palace Yard. (Westminster/Old Palace Yard lay between the Palace of Westminster and Westminster Abbey and was also used frequently as a place of public execution, along with Tyburn and Tower Hill. Sir Walter Raleigh was executed there, as was Guy Fawkes and various others involved with the Gunpowder Plot. Nowadays, an analemmatic sundial given to Queen Elizabeth II by Parliament remains one of the more outstanding features of the area.)

These plots – not to mention the state of the Shrewsbury marriage – led to Mary being given over into the stricter custody of Sir Amyas Paulet. It was at this point that Sir Francis Walsingham, Elizabeth's spymaster supreme, properly enters the picture in regard to Mary's downfall. Walsingham was almost as much an enemy of Mary as was Sir William Cecil, although Elizabeth I never held Walsingham in such high regard, and by the time he died he was almost bankrupt, having had to finance his extensive spy network out of his own pocket. Born around 1532, Walsingham had fled England during the reign of 'Bloody' Mary Tudor, returning when Elizabeth ascended to the throne, whereupon he was rapidly elected to a position in Parliament. His support for the Huguenots in France – French Protestants – meant that he soon found himself working alongside William Cecil in unravelling the various plots against Elizabeth that concerned Mary Queen of Scots. After being transferred to the 'care' of Paulet, Walsingham decided that Mary herself might be needed to weave the web in which he, the spider, would finally entrap her. Firstly, she would need to be lulled into a false sense of security.

Mary's mail and all of her contact with the outside world had by this time been cut off for almost a year, so, when her backdated letters began arriving at her new residence of Chartley Hall, she was understandably delighted. However, little did she realise that this was in fact a prelude to the honey trap correspondence that would allow her to expose herself and thus ensure her arrest and subsequent execution. Having received such a backlog of mail, Mary would thus be convinced that her channels of communication had been reopened, therefore allowing any potential suggestions of rescue to reach her without seeming rather sudden or suspect. To add a further layer to Mary's disenchantment at this point in her imprisonment, her son, James, now an adult and properly ensconced as king of Scotland, had signed a deal with Elizabeth ensuring good relations, with the subtext of a smooth succession for himself to the English throne upon Elizabeth's death; a contract that made no mention of his mother or her current conditions whatsoever. It therefore became clear to Mary that she had been abandoned by the outside world, and that she had nothing to lose. This sense of isolation would serve as the lubricant by which she would slide too readily into the web of Sir Francis Walsingham. All Walsingham needed was for some suitable stooges to come along who would be enamoured enough of the queen of Scots to conceive of a plan to rescue her.

While at Chartley Hall, Mary had been informed by a young Catholic supplicant called Gilbert Gifford – in fact a double agent working for Walsingham – that the brewer who operated out of nearby Burton was willing to help her ferry her messages to the outside world. This would be done by smuggling them inside the beer casks that went to and from the house. Via this secret pipeline, Mary's messages were thus sent to London and into the waiting hands of the latest band of disaffected young Catholic nobles stupid enough to take up her cause (the aforementioned stooges), but not before they were deciphered by Thomas Phelippes, Walsingham's canny codebreaker.

Mary would cross paths with Phelippes during one of his visits to Chartley, during which time she was to remark rather acidly upon the rather displeasing fact of his 'pock-marked face'. Little did she know that he was overseeing virtually all of her correspondence as it crisscrossed the country, settling itself at last in London with the band of disaffected young Catholic nobles. One of those disaffected young Catholic nobles was Anthony Babington, a well-to-do gentleman of Derbyshire origins, who had been recruited by Mary's agent, Thomas Morgan, while they were in France. The same Morgan had also been involved with Sir Francis Throckmorton as part of the Throckmorton Plot. Morgan had in fact once been a member of Mary Queen of Scots' household during the earliest days of her imprisonment in England and had been useful with his 'tip-offs when her rooms were to be searched, help in hiding suspect papers' (Cooper, 2012, p200).

Also backing the Babington Plot was the former Spanish ambassador Bernardino de Mendoza, who had been expelled from England in the wake of failed Throckmorton Plot. Anthony Babington brought with him to the table his entourage of plotting pals, including the poet Chidiock Tichbourne, John Ballard the priest, would-be simpleton-turned-avid assassin John Savage, and various other young disaffected – i.e., bored – Catholic gentlemen who had fallen in love with the image of Mary as a wrongly imprisoned monarch just waiting for a bunch of dashing young bucks to come along and free her.

The group were clumsy enough to commission a portrait of themselves posing for posterity, although thus far this hasn't turned up for historians to pore over. Various woodcuts of their machinations are all that remain in this regard. John Ballard had come over from the Continent and kept the plot warm in London, with John Savage at the helm of the proposed assassination which involved some sketchy method of doing away with Elizabeth by running her through with a sword while she took the air in the gardens at Whitehall Palace (various details in this regard are often confused with particulars of the Parry Plot). The Babington plotters spent a great deal of time soul-searching and drinking in various pubs around the City of London, without ever really realising that their every move was being watched by various shady figures from Walsingham's spy network, including the dermatologically challenged Phelippes.

As the plot was about to pop, double agent Gilbert Gifford promptly fled to the Continent, fearing that he might be caught up in the subsequent fallout and sent to the scaffold as a scapegoat. Beforehand, when Anthony Babington had laid the plot before Mary in a highly incriminating letter, the decipherer Phelippes had added a postscript to her reply so that it appeared that she had asked him to name the 'six gentlemen' who were to carry out the actual assassination of Elizabeth I.

At that point Walsingham pounced, and Mary was arrested while out from Chartley on an abortive hunt. Facing imminent arrest and a troop of Elizabeth's horsemen, she climbed down off her horse, sat on the ground and refused to get up again. She then began fervently to pray and had to be coerced into accompanying Elizabeth's men to the seclusion of nearby Tixall Hall, where she was to spend the next fortnight or so. (All that now remains of this building is the gatehouse, which can be hired out as rather an unusual holiday home). Sir Amyas Paulet then ordered an immediate and thorough search of all her effects back at Chartley Hall, while her secretaries, Nau and Curle, were sent down to London for interrogation, where they proceeded to offer the authorities their full cooperation, thus sparing their lives from the slaughter that was to follow. Mary had by now descended to the absolute nadir of her royal dignity, having Paulet rifling through her coffers and promptly confiscating even her small change and the various keepsakes given her by well-meaning adherents.

Meanwhile, Anthony Babington and the rest of the plotters were rounded up. Babington himself had fled to St John's Wood, where he and several others managed to conceal themselves for a matter of days before they sought help and were discovered. Stories abound that they hid themselves by smearing their faces with walnut oil. They confessed to the entire affair after a variety of tortures, including some rather severe sleep deprivation techniques. John Ballard was so badly racked that he had to be carried to his execution in a chair, with pretty much every joint in his body dislocated.

Elizabeth, shocked by just how close the plot had come to her throne, ordered that the first batch of Babington plotters should suffer a death even more diabolical than the standard traitor's death of being hung, drawn and quartered. However, precise details of exactly what the first batch of Babington plotters thus went through on the scaffold are sparse, although they may have been run through with pitchforks before the usual tortures commenced. In the absence of exact detail, it might be better simply to let the imagination run wild, and to remember that this was a time in history when torture was for the most part considered almost an art form. Despite the threat to their sovereign, the crowds who gathered to watch the executions were, by all accounts, deeply sickened by the spectacle. On hearing of this, a 'tactful' Elizabeth let it be known that the second batch of Babington plotters should be hanged until they were dead, before the traditional sentence of being then drawn and quartered was carried out.

The deaths of the various Babington plotters were perhaps one of the peaks in a slow but steady upsurge in the brutalities carried out against Catholics by the Elizabethan regime. Several months previously, in March, one Margaret Clitherow was brutally put to death in York because of her adherence to the Catholic faith. After having converted to Catholicism in her teens, she was sent to prison for failing to attend church and for not paying the fines associated with such indiscipline; indeed, one of her children was born while she was in prison. She further flouted the law by harbouring various priests, in direct defiance of the Jesuits, etc. Act 1584. This act of Parliament commanded all Roman Catholic priests to leave the country within forty days or else face punishment for high treason, unless they swore an oath of obedience to the queen.

The new law also extended to those who were found to be harbouring such persons who might then face a spell in jail or else perhaps even suffer execution, in order to make an example of them. This was indeed the case with Margaret Clitherow. Her house was already under surveillance by the authorities and so she took to renting a second house several miles away in order to continue her scheme of refuge. When one of her sons travelled to Reims to train for the priesthood, her husband was questioned and the house duly searched, whereupon the priest hole was discovered. Margaret Clitherow was arrested and sentenced to death for the harbouring of Catholic priests, and executed on 25 March, despite being pregnant at the time with her fourth child. She suffered in order to avoid a trial in which her other children would be forced to give evidence and might be tortured during the process of extracting testimony.

The method used to despatch Margaret Clitherow was particularly gruesome. It was a variation of a punishment/inducement often employed within the sphere of the common law legal system, whereby stones were placed upon the chest of the victim until they entered a plea, or else they simply expired. The execution took place in the toll booth at Ouse Bridge, with the two sergeants scheduled to administer the punishment hiring four beggars to perform the onerous duty instead. She was stripped and then a handkerchief was draped across her face. Following this, a sharp rock roughly the size of a fist was laid beneath her. Then her own front door was put on top of her and piled with rocks so that the sharp stone beneath her would break her back. The weight of the rocks needed to perform the execution was said to have been between 700 and 800lb. She suffered for fifteen minutes before perishing, but her body was left for a total of six hours before the door was removed. At some point after her death one of her hands was removed and is now preserved as a relic at the Bar Convent in York. She was canonised by the Catholic Church in 1970.

One person worthy of particular note when it comes to the hounding of Catholics in Elizabeth England around the time that Mary Queen of Scots was arrested is Richard Topcliffe. Born in 1531 in Lincolnshire, he was almost a contemporary of Elizabeth Tudor and well connected at court via various relations, including his uncle, Edward Burgh, who was the first husband of Catherine Parr. Topcliffe participated in some respect in the suppression of the 1569 Northern Rebellion, but he rose to real prominence in the 1580s when he worked tirelessly to help purge England of the 'scourge' of Catholicism. In this respect he very much emulated the example set by Sir Francis Walsingham, practically self-funding his own coterie of what he called 'creatures' to help ferret out papal worshippers wherever he might find them, and like Walsingham he would almost bankrupt himself in the effort.

Once any covert papists found themselves in Topcliffe's clutches they were liable to face various forms of torture in order to induce a confession, or to name and incriminate other culprits. These sessions were carried out either in the Tower of London or sometimes even at Topcliffe's house in Westminster. Such homegrown horrors made him the Protestant reverse of Thomas More, who is said to have 'racked' potential heretics at his house in Chelsea. This is some evidence that Topcliffe even had a special license that permitted him to administer torture under his own roof. Needless to say, Topcliffe's tendency to rack first and secure the facts later soon secured him the most unsavoury of reputations. John Guy said of him that he was 'a vicious, desperately insecure man with pronounced psychopathic tendencies; he was a menacing and divisive figure who almost everyone knew about bur preferred to forget' (Guy, 2016, p170).

He was also a rapist. His victim was Anne Bellamy, a Catholic imprisoned in the Gatehouse Prison at Westminster. In the words of

John Guy, there has been a considerable effort by historians to distance Elizabeth from Topcliffe's activities, but there is more than enough evidence to suggest that she sanctioned and approved of his activities. She knew about the rape and the child it produced, but no action was ever taken against Topcliffe, despite the fact that Anne Bellamy was a prisoner of the crown and thus entitled to protection. The trouble was that Topcliffe was an instrument of the crown, and an essential one at that. For his part, Topcliffe claimed to have rather more intimate knowledge of the queen than her virginal image might suggest. He claimed to have tweaked her nipples and fondled her breasts, as well as foraging up inside her skirts and familiarising himself enough with the details of her vagina to be able to confirm that it was 'the softest' he had ever felt. Such testimony was given by one of Topcliffe's victims, who claimed that he also indulged himself in various sexual fantasies as he racked his victim. When said victim was later executed, Topcliffe demanded that he retract the allegations, which the victim refused to do.

Besides the rack, Topcliffe favoured a form of manacles, with which he would suspend his victim against a wall and leave them to stretch for hours on end. If they passed out from the pain, they would be revived and then the instruments of torture would be readministered. As well as stretching muscles and ligaments to their limits, this form of torture had also the tendency to rupture veins and blood vessels. Richard Topcliffe survived his royal patron only by a year or so, dying in 1604. Some several hundred years later, his first appearance on TV would see him rather incongruously portrayed by *Last of the Summer Wine* actor Brian ('Foggy') Wilde.

Mary Queen of Scots, meanwhile, spent a tense several weeks at Tixall Hall before being taken back to Chartley, but it wasn't long before she was packing up her belongings yet again, in anticipation of what would turn out to be the final move in her long, weary years of imprisonment.

Chapter 43

The Botched Beheading of
Mary Queen of Scots

It has been said many times that nothing became Mary Queen of Scots quite so well as her death: 'In my end is my beginning' and all that. It is undoubtable that she carried it off with near perfect panache, entering into the great hall of Fotheringay Castle – where she had been tried for treason several months previously – draped in her signature black, with a trail of weeping servants in her wake. She then proceeded to unveil herself on the scaffold in an undergarment of Catholic martyr's red. Perhaps that particular dress code was also a sly wink to her reputation as a scarlet woman. The hostile English audience quite possibly took it that way, though it seems unlikely that Mary would have been quite so arch on what was her last day on this earth.

The story leading up to the execution of the queen of Scots is a saga all in itself, with Elizabeth I prevaricating endlessly over the death warrant and then apparently signing it but then denying that she'd ever intended it actually to be used. Or, apparently, not knowing that she'd signed it in the first place, because someone had slipped it between a stack of other official papers while she had other things on her mind. Either way, her Privy Council took it upon themselves to tempt her wrath by having the warrant spirited away to the little village of Fotheringay before she might change her mind again. Thus Mary's fate was sealed whether the queen of England would like it or not. The executioner, Bull, was speedily dispatched to do his duty, staying in a nearby house which can still be seen to this day (the house is adjacent to the entrance to the pathway that leads down to what now remains of the castle). However, anyone wishing to see Fotheringay Castle itself will be dearly disappointed as it was dismantled during the reign of Mary's son, James. All that now remains is a single block of masonry enclosed by an iron fence with a plaque attached to it, as well as various offerings from the general public, including cards and flowers for the executed queen. Fotheringay Castle was also the birthplace of Richard III, who has a separate plaque to himself. The setting, despite the gory legacy, is unsettlingly idyllic.

Mary had been awake for most of the previous night before she was due to be executed, putting her affairs in order and making various bequests to what remained of her household, as well as writing to her family in France, informing them that she was to be despatched like 'a common criminal'. The letter was addressed specifically to Henry III of France, brother of her first husband, Francis, and it reads as follows:

> Sire, my brother-in-law, having by God's will, for my sins I think, thrown myself into the power of the Queen my cousin, at whose hands I have suffered much for almost twenty years, I have finally been condemned to death by her and her Estates. I have asked for my papers, which they have taken away, in order that I might make my will, but I have been unable to recover anything of use to me, or even get leave either to make my will freely or to have my body conveyed after my death, as I would wish, to your kingdom where I had the honour to be queen, your sister and old ally.
>
> Tonight, after dinner, I have been advised of my sentence: I am to be executed like a criminal at eight in the morning. I have not had time to give you a full account of everything that has happened, but if you will listen to my doctor and my other unfortunate servants, you will learn the truth, and how, thanks be to God, I scorn death and vow that I meet it innocent of any crime, even if I were their subject. The Catholic faith and the assertion of my God-given right to the English crown are the two issues on which I am condemned, and yet I am not allowed to say that it is for the Catholic religion that I die, but for fear of interference with theirs. The proof of this is that they have taken away my chaplain, and although he is in the building, I have not been able to get permission for him to come and hear my confession and give me the Last Sacrament, while they have been most insistent that I receive the consolation and instruction of their minister, brought here for that purpose. The bearer of this letter and his companions, most of them

your subjects, will testify to my conduct at my last hour. It remains for me to beg Your Most Christian Majesty, my brother-in-law and old ally, who have always protested your love for me, to give proof now of your goodness on all these points: firstly by charity, in paying my unfortunate servants the wages due them – this is a burden on my conscience that only you can relieve: further, by having prayers offered to God for a queen who has borne the title Most Christian, and who dies a Catholic, stripped of all her possessions. As for my son, I commend him to you in so far as he deserves, for I cannot answer for him. I have taken the liberty of sending you two precious stones, talismans against illness, trusting that you will enjoy good health and a long and happy life. Accept them from your loving sister-in-law, who, as she dies, bears witness of her warm feeling for you. Again I commend my servants to you. Give instructions, if it please you, that for my soul's sake part of what you owe me should be paid, and that for the sake of Jesus Christ, to whom I shall pray for you tomorrow as I die, I be left enough to found a memorial mass and give the customary alms.

This Wednesday, two hours after midnight.

Your very loving and most true sister, Mary R. To the most Christian king, my brother-in-law and old ally.

It was early in the morning when the knock came on the door to her rooms, and soon after that she was being escorted down to the great hall by a train of attendants, some of whom were, as said, already weeping and lamenting the impending loss. The moment has been immortalised on canvas more times than one cares to mention. Woodwork and masonry purported to have been fashioned from the staircase Mary made use of on her final descent in Fotheringay are now said to be in evidence in the structure of the Talbot Hotel in nearby Oundle. Of particular note is the indentation in the wood of the staircase, said to have been made by the impression of Mary's ring as she forced her fingers into the woodwork, either to escape or else to leave a little something for posterity. She would have needed the biceps of the Incredible Hulk to have performed such a feat, though there are still those willing to believe the tale. It seems a far safer bet to accept that a greater part of the stonework of the Talbot Hotel does indeed consist of Fotheringay Castle fragments.

Back in 1587, attempts were made to separate Mary from her loyal household as she mounted the scaffold in the crowded great hall, but she protested and as a result was allowed to keep a small selection of servants to wait upon her, but only on the condition that they not dip their handkerchiefs in her spilled blood to use as relics. They were also to keep their lamentations to a minimum, for fear of disturbing the guards who were posted around the hall, not to mention the 'guests' themselves.

A large fire was roaring in the fireplace nearby, heating an apparently bright but chilly early February morning. Such good weather was taken as a sign that the servants of England were indeed embarking upon a noble endeavour in despatching one of the country's most fervent foes. There was by all accounts an almost serene calm about the prisoner: 'the queen listened patiently while the commission for her execution was read aloud. Her expression never changed. Cecil's own official observer, Robert Wise, commented later that from her detached regard, she might even have been listening to a pardon, rather than the warrant for her own death' (Fraser, 2009, p668).

Mary's old custodian, the Earl of Shrewsbury, was present, as was the Earl of Kent, and between them they directed the proceedings, with the odd little sour intervention from Sir Amyas Paulet. Mary made herself comfortable in a chair while she listened to these sermons. (The same chair is now alleged to be the same one that sits all but forgotten in All Saints Church in Conington. The church is abandoned but the key can be obtained from a house in the nearby village for anyone who wishes to go and take a look.)

Almost as soon as Mary had made herself comfortable, the Dean of Peterborough launched into a long sermon during which he exhorted her to abandon the Catholic faith and convert to Protestantism, but Mary remained steadfast. This was her last big mortal moment and absolutely no one was going to spoil it for her. As the Dean of Peterborough began to pray, so too did she, only she was praying in rather vociferous Latin, and from there it sort of degenerated into a rather unedifying spectacle of the two of them raising their voices louder and louder in an effort to be heard.

Mary then began to prepare herself for the execution itself, at which point Bull the executioner and his assistant tried to help themselves to the rosary she was wearing, which they were entitled to under their traditional role of executioners. Mary pulled it away from them and made it clear that it, and various other of her garments, had already been promised to her ladies, but that they would be recompensed via monetary means. She then made a rather wry remark that she had never before had such grooms of the chamber to attend on her, as she was forced to shed most of her heavier outer garments, revealing the 'scandalous' undergarment of Catholic martyr's red beneath. This moment has been portrayed on the screen in almost every film or TV adaptation of Mary's life, with varying degrees of success. Those unaware of the Catholic martyr connotations were perhaps doubtless left wondering whether or not she was simply making some sort of a morbid fashion statement.

Jane Kennedy and Elizabeth Curle were the two women who had been allowed to ascend the scaffold with her, and as they fixed the sleeves to the red dress and made other necessary adjustments they wept uncontrollably. Mary consoled them not to sob for her, saying to them that the end to all of her earthly troubles was imminent. A silk handkerchief was then tied around her eyes and she either knelt before the small block or was led over to it, in a vague echo of the fumbled execution of Lady Jane Grey.

Mary was again praying when the first blow of the axe struck, missing her neck completely and instead coming down somewhere close to the back of her head. Several witnesses said she gasped aloud but others stated that she remained quite silent as Bull quickly corrected his mistake and almost took her head clean off with a second blow. A small strand of sinew remained after this and he used his axe to saw through it, before then picking up the severed head and holding it before the crowd.

The already botched execution now turned into macabre farce as the wig that Mary had been wearing – and which is all that Bull was actually holding onto – now detached itself from her head, allowing the decapitated head to tumble down onto the scaffold, whereupon it almost rolled away, leaving the bemused Bull holding the wig in his outstretched hand. Mary's actual hair was at that point revealed to be grey and cut short; long gone were the lustrous reddish-brown locks of legend.

At that point, as Bull's assistant went to pull off Mary's garters to claim them, her little Skye Terrier crawled out from underneath them and went and placed itself piteously between the severed head and the body of its mistress. It was taken away and washed clean of her blood but pined away, eventually dying of a broken heart. Of all the various tales told in regard to Mary's execution, this is the one that seems the most problematic. While being an ardent animal lover, it seems a considerable stretch of credibility to imagine that Mary would have reached the scaffold from her rooms on another floor of Fotheringay Castle without treading on the poor little creature as it struggled to remain concealed and also to match pace with her. What seems far more likely is that the terrier might have leapt forth from the arms of a faithful watching servant and taken refuge between the already dead body and the severed head. However, as with so much concerning all aspects of Mary's astonishing life, the original version isn't entirely out of the question either.

Mary's severed head was then taken by Bull to one of the windows of the great hall and held up for the benefit of the crowds outside. Another version of the story says that it was then displayed on a black velvet cushion for some several hours before it was finally retrieved, just in case anyone suspected that there was some sort of a cover-up (the general public of the time were not a particularly trusting bunch where matters of state security were concerned).

The block on which Mary had been executed was duly burned, as were all of the clothes she had been wearing, the scaffold structure, and indeed anything else that might be used as a relic by her followers. Such stringent measures by the Tudor authorities have had the unfortunate side-effect of making a mockery – some 400 or so years later – of the various items of clothing on display in stately homes around England that are purported to have been worn by the queen at her execution. The point of these eradications was that Mary was to become a 'non-person' in the wake of her execution, hence her burial in the relatively distant (from the hallowed burial site at Westminster Abbey, that is) surroundings of Peterborough Cathedral, and certainly the authorities weren't going to be leaving anything to chance with any of the leftovers, no matter how innocuous any of these 'relics' may now appear to modern eyes. The fact that Fotheringay Castle itself was within fifty years or so effectively razed to the ground might also serve to underline this point, although the slow destruction of that particular historic monument may not have begun with that end in mind; several accounts say that it fell away more due to natural neglect than through any orchestrated campaign of destruction.

Mary's body was eventually removed from the great hall and wrapped in the cloth from her billiard table, while her attendants were prevented from seeing it and paying a final tribute. Their incarceration at Fotheringay Castle then continued for some several months before they were released, at which point they were able to spread the truth about Mary's execution as opposed to the spin put about by the Elizabethan government. It is quite possible that some of the more fanciful legends surrounding the event may have originated with these loyal adherents, but there were numerous eyewitnesses to the botched fact of the beheading itself, so this at least can be held in no doubt.

After the execution Mary's body was embalmed, and the internal organs were taken out and then either burnt or – according to yet *another* legend – buried in a casket which still resides somewhere in the remains of the castle mound, or in the surrounding grassland on the castle site. (There is a caravan park very close by, so it seems rather unnerving to imagine various holidaymakers roasting their hot dogs several feet above the earthly remains of Mary Queen of Scots.) Her body was then placed in a sturdy coffin comprised of oak and lead and left in the great hall, presumably until such time as it would be taken to Peterborough Cathedral for burial. It remained there while the general mourning across Europe for Mary Queen of Scots had passed, as well as the possibility of any serious reprisals from the various foreign powers. Eventually, the coffin was taken by night in a solemn procession to Peterborough Cathedral, where she was laid to rest in a tomb almost directly adjacent to that other imprisoned, tragic Catholic queen, Catherine of Aragon. The entire ceremony cost a total of £321, and as usual Elizabeth I did not attend, sending the Countess of Bedford as her official representative.

Mary remained at rest in Peterborough Abbey until 1612, when her son, James, was on the throne of England as James I. He had his mother's remains removed and taken down to London where they were reinterred in Westminster Abbey, in a chapel adjacent to Elizabeth's. James had a grand monument built for his mother, one that far surpassed in splendour the tomb that Elizabeth I now shared with her half-sister Mary. The fact that Mary Queen of Scots had, before her death, expressly requested that she be buried in France seemed not to matter one whit to James, nor the fact that she had also said that she did not want to be buried near any of her ancestors, i.e., Henry VII. And one can only imagine that she would have positively baulked at the idea that she might end up being laid to rest a mere stone's throw from the woman who ordered her execution.

Mary's tomb has since become renowned as a 'place of miracles', but she now also shares her final resting space with countless of her Stuart descendants. However, appearances mattered a great deal to Mary, and one might imagine with a wry smile the fact that her tomb is indeed far grander than that of her 'dear cousin'. The Marie Stuart Society attend the tomb every year on or around the date of her birth and fresh flowers are placed there. The bars of the tomb are opened to allow the offering to be placed inside. This author had the privilege of placing the flowers on one such occasion, getting about as close to Mary's earthly remains as anyone from the general public is ever likely to do.

Several death masks purporting to be of Mary currently reside in various places of Marian interest around the country, but they are to be approached rather hesitantly, to say the least. A death mask is an impression made of wax or plaster, taken of the face of the deceased shortly after they have died, with the express purpose of preserving their features for posterity. However, death masks are not the most reliable of indicators as to a person's features, given that the weight of the wax or plaster had a tendency to distort the face somewhat. This is on top of the fact that the muscles of the face would either clench during death or else relax to a point where the subject might become almost unrecognisable.

As far as Mary Queen of Scots was concerned, the point was that no relics or mementoes whatsoever were to be retained after her demise, hence the extreme unlikelihood that one of those rather macabre keepsakes was ever made. The death masks that are in circulation – and there are several – look rather more like Katherine Hepburn than they do Mary Stuart, which indicates that the maker may have had an eye more on the 1936 movie *Mary of Scotland* than on the real, and rather more aquiline, profile of the deceased Scots queen. What this basically denotes is that the likelihood of any of the death masks being genuine is almost zero; one simply did not attempt to preserve for posterity the countenance of an executed traitor. That said, one can quite imagine Elizabeth I ordering such a mask to be made simply so that she might see what her 'dear cousin' actually looked like in the flesh, though this also seems unlikely. Nineteen years of imprisonment had ravaged Mary's once-legendary beauty, so for Elizabeth's monumental vanity such an exercise would have been a pyrrhic victory at best.

Chapter 44

The Armada Attacks

The English victory over the marauding Spanish Armada in 1588 is seen as one of the greatest – if not perhaps *the* greatest – victories of the whole Elizabethan epoch. Elizabeth I's popularity ratings went through the roof in the wake of the rout, which saw the mighty galleons of the Catholic Phillip II limping back to Spain with the majority of the crews either dead or dying, and with the Pope himself commenting that Elizabeth was indeed a formidable foe and how much more marvellous it would be if only she were to become a Catholic herself.

But the English victory over the Spanish was very much down to luck, and had little at all to do with the skill of the English or because of any sort of superior firepower. Had the wind been blowing in another direction then the outcome could have been very different, and Elizabeth might have been gracing the executioner's block on Tower Green instead of having a commemorative portrait painted for posterity. Also, in truth, the attack could not have come at a worse time for the country: 'The simple truth was that England was poorly prepared both militarily and financially for the fight. Its limited resources of men and money were already committed in the Low Countries. Royal coffers could not hope to pay for those troops and sailors waiting for the Duke of Parma to arrive' (Alford, 2012, p254).

The cold war that had existed between the Protestant queen of England and her Catholic former brother-in-law, Phillip II of Spain, finally erupted into all-out war in 1588. Perhaps the execution of Mary Queen of Scots was the last straw for Phillip, the champion of Catholicism, but he had in fact been building and planning his armada for several years ahead of her death, and Mary's many pleas for his help during her long imprisonment had fallen on either deaf or extremely indecisive ears. Mary had pleaded to him several times for help, all to no avail.

Perhaps more pertinently, the Spanish may have wanted revenge on Sir Francis Drake, Elizabeth's spectacular seaman, for his calamitous raid on Cadiz in 1587, which had temporarily crippled the fledgling enterprise. Whether or not Drake really was playing a game of bowls at Plymouth when the armada itself was sighted in 1588, and determined to those onlookers that he would finish his game before he leapt into action is probably apocryphal, but it still sounds good to your average impressionable English schoolchild.

The English fleet was anchored at Plymouth at the time but the Spanish did not begin their campaign by launching a direct attack on it. Instead, they progressed slowly and were sighted off the Lizard in Cornwall on 19 July 1588. The fleet was captained by the Duke Medina Sidonia, perhaps not the best man to be left in charge of the great enterprise, given his lack of military experience and a tendency to seasickness, at the very least. Under his command there were several skirmishes, but the fleet was unable to take any sort of a foothold and had to return to Calais to regroup. It was here that the spectacular surprise attack of the English fire ships scattered them completely. A fire ship was an empty vessel filled with highly flammable materials which was then ignited and sailed toward the enemy ships, with the crew escaping by means of a secreted smaller vessel beforehand. The swiftness and surprise of this attack meant that the armada was unable to rendezvous with the Duke of Parma's army. Parma was governor of the Spanish Netherlands and was to spearhead the land invasion of England, but the poor coordination between him and Sidonia meant that the Battle of Gravelines – the attack of the English fire ships – put paid to this idea completely, as well as the fact that Parma's army was stifled by the presence of Dutch flyboats.

What was left of the Spanish armada fled north, with the English ships not far behind and in hot pursuit. Storms wrecked what was left of Phillip II's mighty enterprise, and many of his ships were washed up off the coasts of Scotland and Ireland, where countless stranded crew members were slaughtered by the natives. Those who avoided this ignoble fate faced a slow, arduous crawl back to their own country, with many perishing from starvation in the process. The fate of the winners was not much better, all things considered. With the threat from the Spanish having passed, those sailors who survived were left to their own devices with little or no recompense. As a result, sickness and starvation soon became widespread among their ranks as they gathered in places such as Margate, where it was said that the bodies were literally piling up in the streets.

It was shortly after the Battle of Gravelines that Elizabeth I went to Tilbury to rally her troops. She wore some sort of armour, or at the very least the breastplate from a suit of armour, and rode back and forth among her troops on horseback, where she then proceeded to deliver perhaps the most famous of all of her many soundbite speeches:

> My loving people, we have been persuaded by some that are careful of our safety to take heed how we commit ourselves to armed multitudes for fear of treachery; but I assure you, I do not desire to live to distrust my faithful and loving people. Let tyrants fear. I have always so behaved myself that, under God, I have placed my chiefest strength and safe guard in the loyal hearts and good will of my subjects, and therefore I am come amongst you, as you see, at this time, not for my recreation and disport, but being resolved, in the midst and heat of the battle, to live or die amongst you all, to lay down my life for my God and for my kingdom and for my people, my honour, and my blood, even in the dust. I know I have the body of a weak and feeble woman, but I have the heart and stomach of a king, and a king of England too, and think foul scorn that Parma or Spain, or any prince of Europe should dare to invade the borders of my realm; the which, rather than any dishonour shall grow by me, I myself will take up arms, I myself will be your general, judge, and rewarder of every one of your virtues in the field. I know, already for your forwardness, you have deserved rewards and crowns; and we do assure you, in the word of a prince, they shall be duly paid you. In the meantime my lieutenant-general shall be in my stead, than whom never prince commanded a more noble or worthy subject, not doubting but by your obedience to my general, by your concord in the camp, and your valour in the field, we shall shortly have a famous victory over those enemies of my God, of my kingdom, and of my people.

As she made this speech, she was guarded and escorted by her favourite – and perhaps also the love of her life – Robert Dudley, the Earl of Leicester. Not long after the threat from the armada had been vanquished, he journeyed to Buxton to take the curative waters, but died during a stopover at Oxford. For Elizabeth, therefore, the victory over her former brother-in-law was tinged with the tragedy of losing her favourite courtier. In fact, so disturbed was she by the loss that she locked herself in her apartments for several days, until finally the doors were broken down and she was summoned back to life. The letter that Leicester had written to her shortly before he died she was to keep in a treasure box by her bed, where it was found after her death, marked simply 'His last letter'.

Chapter 45

The Only Way is Essex:
Elizabeth I's Tempestuous Toyboy

Robert Devereux, the 2nd Earl of Essex, was the stepson of Elizabeth I's favourite Robert Dudley, and like his stepfather he was also tall, dynamic and rather dashing. Therefore, it didn't take him too long to catch the ageing queen's eye and shoehorn himself into the Robert Dudley-sized hole that had been left with the death of her beloved Earl of Leicester in 1588.

Pretty soon the royal spinster was openly besotted with her new court favourite, who could do no wrong in her eyes, despite the fact that he had an annoying habit of rubbing almost everyone else up the wrong way. Besides walloping Walter Raleigh out of the way, and making an enemy of the Cecil faction, the real problem was that Essex had an ego, and a pretty hefty one at that. He was prone to storming out of court when he didn't get his way, and on one occasion he even drew his sword on the queen after she threatened to box his ears for the effrontery of turning his back on her. Such a slight coming from anyone else should have seen them being sent straight to the Tower, but instead Essex was able to slouch off in another of his famous huffs, quite untouchable by the sheer virtue of being so buff. Such slights, however, counted for a very great deal in the eyes of his enemies, particularly the aforementioned Cecil faction, who sought to stymie his chances of real promotion and influence at the court. Essex was always after military glory too, but his expeditions were frequently inept or wasteful from a financial point of view. Most of them were punctuated by various scolding letters from Elizabeth chastising him for wasting men, money, and resources in a pointless pursuit of glory. She was frequently indulgent of his aspirations, but even her besotted patience had a limit, as he was soon to discover.

After a protracted campaign in Ireland during which he privately parlayed with the Earl of Tyrone, the leader of the Irish discontents, Essex returned to England to face his detractors and burst in on the queen at Nonsuch Palace, early in the morning. On this occasion, Elizabeth was without benefit of either her wig or the shedloads of make-up she then wore to hide her ageing countenance. Despite the shock she kept her cool and managed to keep Essex talking until her household staff were able to take control of the situation and usher him from her presence.

Quite what Essex himself thought about finding his sovereign in such a state of undress was soon to be voiced, and rather indiscreetly at that. Essex was put under house arrest for his insolence and went on trial shortly afterwards. As a result, he lost all of his offices and privileges and was put into a state of confinement, to await the queen's pleasure. It was at this juncture that he began to lose what little sense of reason remaining to him, openly declaring that the queen's mind was 'as crooked as her carcase', and falsely giving voice to the idea that he was in fact more popular than her and had a right thusly to wrench her away from what he saw as a corrupt nest of councillors – i.e., the Cecil faction.

On the 8 February 1601 he led an open rebellion on the streets of London, originating from his base in Essex House on the Strand. However, far from receiving the wholehearted support from the public that had followed him for much of his early career, the common people turned their backs on his foolishness and slammed their doors in his face. As a result, the rebellion petered out as quickly as it had begun, and the rebels were forced to retreat back to the relative safety of Essex House.

Throughout this storm in a Tudor teacup the queen's resolve never faltered: 'When a false alarm reached the Court that the City had revolted, she was no more amazed "than she would have been to hear of a fray in Fleet Street". "She would have gone out in person to see what any rebel of them all durst do against her, had not her councillors with much ado stayed her"' (Neale, 1960, p378). Not long after this, there was a short standoff between the rebels and the queen's men, and then Essex and his compatriots surrendered and were once more placed under arrest. This time there were to be no reprieves, no matter how much he might try flashing his well-rounded calves.

Essex was tried for treason and sentenced to death. During the days of his imprisonment, army captain Thomas Lee hatched a plot to imprison Elizabeth I in her bedchamber until she relented and released Essex, but he was caught before the plan could be put into effect. Lee had served alongside Essex in Ireland, but was tried and put to death the very next day for his affrontery. Essex himself was beheaded on 25 February on Tower Green, with a reported three strokes of the axe being required to remove his pretty head from his shoulders. His executioner, Thomas Derrick, had been convicted of rape but had been pardoned by none other than the Earl of Essex himself, on the condition that he became an executioner at Tyburn, not a post that enjoyed a great deal of prestige given that it could clearly be meted out as some sort of punishment. As previously mentioned, executioners often found themselves under threat of attack from the families of those they had either already dispatched or were shortly about to.

There is a legend, in fact almost entirely apocryphal, surrounding the death of the Earl of Essex, one which states that he had in his possession a ring given to him by the queen and which, if returned to her, meant that he desired her help above all things. In this case he is said to have given it to one of her ladies while he was a prisoner in the Tower, hoping that as a result it would be returned to Elizabeth and she would show mercy on him and instantly lift the sentence of execution. The ring fell – quite literally by all accounts – into the hands of one Lady Scrope, a distant relative of the queen, who sent it by a messenger boy to be given to the queen. Unfortunately, so the tale goes, the ring instead fell into the hands of her sister, the Countess of Nottingham. The sway of her husband, an implacable foe of Essex, swiftly made sure that the ring never reached the hands of the queen, and so poor Essex went to his execution with his plea for mercy apparently unanswered. The tragic tale concludes with the epilogue that when Elizabeth was visiting the dying Countess of Nottingham, the countess confessed to what had happened, and that in a rage Elizabeth struck her and then cried out 'God may forgive you but I never can!'

The demise of the Earl of Essex was seen as one of those blows from which an aged soul might not recover. Elizabeth I had seen almost all of her favourites – Dudley, Hatton and Cecil, as well as the disgraced Essex – perish before her, and the last straw may have come when she bade farewell to the aforementioned Countess of Nottingham, who was the niece of her cousin Lady Knollys. Following on from this latest loss, Elizabeth retreated to the sanctuary of Richmond Palace, from which she was never to emerge. She became increasingly melancholic and paranoid, either roaming about the place seeking out unseen enemies –

sometimes hacking away behind a hanging drape with a nearby sword – or else simply sitting on a pile of cushions for hours on end, reportedly with her finger in her mouth. Eventually, she was persuaded to take to her bed, during which time she drifted in and out of consciousness. It was said that an ulcer in her throat that had made eating difficult burst during this time, bringing some relief, but it was not enough for her to rally sufficiently. She died between 2am and 3am on 24 March 1603.

Bibliography

Ackroyd, Peter, 2012, *The History of England Volume II: Tudors*, London, Macmillan.

Alford, Stephen, 2012, *The watchers*, London: Penguin Books.

Baldwin Smith, Lacey, 1969, *The Elizabethan epic*, London: Panther Books.

Baldwin Smith, Lacey, 2010, *Catherine Howard*, Stroud: Amberley.

Bingham, Caroline, 1995, *Darnley*, London: Constable and Company Limited.

Bruce, Marie Louise, 1972, *Anne Boleyn*, London: Collins.

Cooper, John, 2012, *The Queen's agent – Francis Walsingham at the Court of Elizabeth I*, London: Faber and Faber.

Denny, Joanna, 2008, *Katherine Howard*, London: Piatkus Books Ltd.

Doran, Susan, 2007, *Mary Queen of Scots – an illustrated life*, London: The British Library.

Dunn, Jane, 2004, *Elizabeth & Mary*, London: Harper Perennial.

Edwards, Francis, 1964, *The dangerous queen*, London: Geoffrey Chapman.

Fox, Julia, 2008, *Jane Boleyn*, London: Phoenix.

Fraser, Antonia, 1993, *The six wives of Henry VIII*, London: Phoenix Press.

Fraser, Antonia, 2009, *Mary Queen of Scots (40th anniversary edition)*, London: Phoenix.

Graham, Roderick, 2009, *An accidental tragedy – the life of Mary, Queen of Scots*, Edinburgh: Birlinn.

Gregory, Philippa, 2011, *The other queen*, London: HarperCollins.

Guy, John, 2009, *My heart is my own: the life of Mary Queen of Scots*, London: Fourth Estate.

Guy, John, 2017, *Elizabeth – the forgotten years*, London: Penguin Books.

Haynes, Alan 2004, *The Elizabethan secret services*, Stroud: Sutton Publishing

Hilton, Lisa, 2014, *Elizabeth – renaissance prince*, London: Weidenfeld & Nicolson.

Ives, Eric, 2004, *The life and death of Anne Boleyn*, Oxford: Blackwell Publishing.

Jenkins, Elizabeth, 1965, *Elizabeth the great*, London: University Paperbacks.

Lacey, Robert, 1972, *Henry VIII*, London: Book Club Associates.

Lindsey, Karen, 1995, *Divorced, beheaded, survived*, USA: Da Capo Press.

Lipscomb, Suzannah, 2009, *1536*, Oxford: Lion.

Lovell, Mary S., 2006, *First lady of Chatsworth – Bess of Hardwick*, London: Abacus.

Mackay, James, 2000, *In my end is my beginning – a life of Mary Queen of Scots*, Edinburgh: Mainstream Publishing.

Neale, J.E., 1960, *Queen Elizabeth I*, Middlesex: Penguin Books.

Norton, Elizabeth, 2009, *Jane Seymour*, Stroud: Amberley Publishing.

Plaidy, Jean, 1978, *Mary Queen of Scots*, London: W.H.Allen & Co. Ltd.

Plowden, Alison, 2010, *Two queens in one isle*, Stroud: The History Press.

Plowden, Alison, 2013, *Danger to Elizabeth*, Stroud: The History Press.

Porter, Linda, 2010, *Katherine the queen – the remarkable life of Katherine Parr*, London: Macmillan.

Porter, Linda, 2013, *Crown of thistles*, London: Macmillan.

Read, Conyers, 1965, *Mr Secretary Cecil and Queen Elizabeth*, London: Jonathan Cape.

Ridley, Jasper, 2002, *A brief history of the Tudor age*, London: Constable & Robinson Ltd.

Ridley, Jasper, *Elizabeth I*, London: Penguin Books.

Ross, Josephine, 2005, *The men who would be king*, London: Phoenix.

Somerset, Anne, 1997, *Elizabeth I*, London: Phoenix.

Starkey, David, 2004, *Six wives – the queens of Henry VIII*, London: Vintage Books.

Tweedie, David, 2006, *David Rizzio & Mary Queen of Scots*, Stroud: Sutton Publishing.

Warnicke, Retha, 1989, *The rise and fall of Anne Boleyn*, Cambridge: Cambridge University Press.

Warnicke, Retha, 2006, *Mary Queen of Scots*, Abingdon: Routledge.

Weir, Alison, 2007, *The six wives of Henry VIII*, London: Vintage Books.

Weir, Alison, 2008, *Henry VIII – king and court*, London: Vintage Books.

Weir, Alison, 2008, *Elizabeth the queen*, London: Vintage Books.

Weir, Alison, 2009, *The lady in the Tower: The fall of Anne Boleyn*, London: Jonathan Cape.

Weir, Alison, 2011, *Mary Boleyn – 'the great and infamous whore'*, London: Jonathan Cape.

Zweig, Stefan, 2011, *Mary Stuart*, London: Pushkin Press.

Index

Index